The Metamorphosis of Love

by
Ivor A. Toney

The Metamorphosis of Love

Contents

Chapter 1:
Acknowledgments

In this journey to demystify the essence and misconceptions surrounding love, I extend sincere gratitude to my Lord and Saviour, Jesus Christ, who illuminated me with insights and experiences. I thank Him for the grace to continue, empowerment to endure, and tenacity to persevere in life's most difficult experiences. Because of Your unbending support and daily guidance, those experiences have enabled me to embark upon the quest for truth, hence this script. As such, this exploration isn't just a product of solitary musings but a tapestry woven from the collective wisdom of those You empowered to question, love, and serve through the example You set while You walked this earth.

I must acknowledge my many mentors, including Principal Alvi, Pastor DeSouza, and Dr. E. Joseph, who guided my understanding and enlivened my imagination.

To my critics, you've sharpened my thoughts, and therefore, to you, I owe the vibrancy of these pages. Your contributions have been the beacon that illuminated the intricate corridors of love's manifold expressions.

To Adnan and the West Humber Crew, unwittingly, you have added intricate strands to the tapestry of this mosaic in monumental ways. From the consistent encouragements to pursue excellence to the candid conversations about observed abilities, all have had an unforgettable, memorable effect on what is memorialized on these pages.

Chapter 2:
Dedications

I Dedicate these profound renderings to:
God, firstly, for His mercy, grace, and guidance.

My loving wife Dianne, thank you for your love and unbending support throughout the last 30 years of marriage. Your generosity, sticktoitiveness, and commitment have been a comfort and grounding force, reminding me of love's most fundamental lessons.

My Children:

Shanice, Elisha, Ivor, Stephanie, ShannaKay, Trisha, Denzil, Krishana, Carltaya, Rhoda, Xyeisha, Via, Nayma, and Shane.

Grandchildren:

Brea, Ja'niya, Orian, Shaniya, and Levi

Thank you all for your unparalleled/unconditional love. You have all contributed to these pages in a variety of ways. As you traverse this exceptional and incomparable experience called life, I pray that you will consistently challenge yourself by acting with wisdom. In this context, wisdom refers to a mindfulness approach to life in which one acts with knowledge while simultaneously doubting what is known. This, then, would enable you to pursue truth daily and critically analyze information with the understanding that knowledge informs actions.

My Little Brother J.D., Sister StaceyAnn, Roxan, and Andria. Thank you for your willingness to give unconditionally and for inspiring me to do better, be better, push harder, and dream bigger.

You, the readers who loved intensely, served unconditionally and felt the pangs of misconceived love, to the tireless seekers of truth, who've pondered over coffee-stained pages in the quiet hours of the night, questioning whether love is a feeling that captivates or a service that liberates. To you who stand at the crossroads of love and sacrifice, this chapter opens its arms, inviting not just contemplation but an active engagement with love's genuine essence. As we venture deeper into the heart's mazes, remember it is for you, the brave ones willing to dismantle years of myths for the jewel of true love, that these words are woven, meant to rekindle the spirit and illuminate the paths of those daring enough to question, to voluntarily, sacrificially serve, and to love authentically.

Introduction

Love is perhaps the most celebrated yet mystified in the maze of human emotions. We explore love not to diminish its wonder but to illuminate the misconceptions that often cloud its true essence. In doing so, we aim to unravel the complex weave of perceptions, ideologies, and experiences that define love across cultures, time, and individual hearts.

Love, in its purest form, is a mystery that has captivated poets, philosophers, and prophets alike. It has been immortalized in sonnets, scriptures, and the silent gestures of everyday life. Yet, for all its omnipresence, the proper understanding of love remains as elusive as ever. Does love manifest merely as a spectrum of feelings, or does it transcend the emotional realm to embody acts of voluntary sacrificial serving?

The quest to highlight the misconceptions about love is not taken lightly. It requires peering beyond the veil of society's idealizations, navigating the murky waters of cultural norms, and confronting the illusions perpetuated by literature and media. It calls for a deep introspection into our own hearts and the roles we play in the theatre of love.

Across the ages, love has been depicted in diverse forms, each reflecting the guiding beliefs of its time. The ancient poets described love as a divine madness, powerful enough to topple kingdoms and defy deity. In contrast, contemporary narratives often equate love with happiness, fulfillment, and personal completion, subtly intertwining it with notions of self-gratification and pleasure.

We seek to decipher love's true meaning through a blend of persuasive narratives, descriptive insights, motivational dialogues, and inspirational stories. Is love the emotional whirlwind that sweeps us off our feet, or is it the steady hand that guides us through the storm? Is it found in the grand gestures of passion or the quiet acts of kindness that go unnoticed?

This exploration is not merely academic; it is profoundly personal. At some point or another, each of us has grappled with love's mysteries. We have basked in its warmth and shivered in its absence. We have been the givers of love and its recipients, often navigating the delicate balance between the two. Through this journey, we seek to unearth the depths of love's many facets, not just as an emotion but as a principle that guides human conduct.

In the following chapters, we will dissect societal expectations of love, traverse its portrayals in literature and media, and analyze the philosophical underpinnings that have shaped our understanding of love through the ages. We delve into the cultural evolution of love, challenging the myths and idealizations that have distorted its true nature.

Moreover, we distinguish between self-love and narcissism, explore the significance of compassionate love, and examine love as a choice and an act of service. We investigate the lifecycle of love in relationships, highlighting the transition from infatuation to maturity and underscoring the foundational role of communication in nurturing love.

It is a testament to love's complexity that it encompasses such a broad spectrum of experiences and expressions. From the passionate intensity of romantic love to the steadfast devotion of agape love, each form offers a unique lens through which to view the human heart.

In dissecting the misconceptions of love, we aspire not only to clarify what love is not but to celebrate what it can be. We challenge the reader to look beyond the conventional portrayals of love, question the societal scripts handed down through generations, and discover a more authentic, serving, and transformative understanding of love.

Let us then embark on this journey with open hearts and minds, ready to confront the myths, embrace the truths, and rediscover love in its most genuine form. In the exploration of love's mysteries, we find not only the essence of humanity but the pathway to our own hearts.

This book, therefore, serves as a guide on this quest for understanding. It is a declaration that love, in its most profound form, is not merely a feeling but a manner of living—one that elevates serving to the pinnacle of its expression. In love's purest form, to serve is to love, and to love is to serve.

And so, as we sift through the layers and peel back the curtains, we may find that love, in its varying expressions, serves as the sincerest testament to our humanity. It is the bridge that connects, the light that illuminates, and the force that empowers us to transcend our limitations.

With this understanding, we set forth, seeking not just to define love but to embody it in our actions, words, and lives. Let this exploration be a beacon, guiding us toward a more compassionate, comprehensive, and authentic love. A love that nurtures, heals, and unites. A love that voluntarily and sacrificially serves.

Chapter 3:
What Is Love?

The quest to unveil the essence of love often sends us spiraling into an abyss of clichés, tales, and misconceptions. Is love the heart racing, palms sweating, the thrill of a first kiss, or a partner's quiet, steadfast presence in the darkest of times? We're taken on this philosophical journey not to disassemble love into its bare components but to expand our comprehension, encompassing the manifold ways it is manifested and understood across cultures and centuries. This dive into love's true meaning challenges the societal blueprint of romantic love, urging us to consider it not merely as a series of emotional responses but as a dynamic, serving force. In its purest form, love emerges not as an entity bound by the shackles of expectation but as a transformative power transcending mere feelings. It teaches us to voluntarily and sacrificially serve, to give without the intention of receiving, to understand profoundly, and to empathize fully. By exploring love through the lenses of societal expectations, philosophical inquiries, and diverse cultural definitions, we embark on a reflective expedition to decipher love's multifaceted character. Let's move beyond the surface, exploring the depths where love is not just felt but actively made and remade in the furnace of life's trials and triumphs.

Societal Expectations of Love In our exploration of love, we must turn our gaze toward the invisible chains that shape our perceptions and experiences of love: societal expectations. Often subtle yet profoundly influential, these societal norms and ideals paint a picture of idyllic and unattainable love, setting the stage for disillusionment.

In the tapestry of human culture, love has been adorned with various hues and textures. Society, like an artist with a brush, creates broad strokes that define what love should look like, feel like, and how it should evolve. These expectations are not merely whispers in the wind but loud proclamations that resonate through every relationship stage.

Consider the fairy tales of childhood, with their promises of 'happily ever after.' From an early age, we are fed narratives that love is a rescuing force capable of overcoming any adversity without effort or conflict. This portrayal is a double-edged sword, inspiring yet misleading, nurturing hope but fostering unrealistic standards.

Through the societal lens, love often assumes the form of grand gestures and eternal passion. Yet, such depictions overlook the mundane yet meaningful expressions of love: a shared silence, the comfort of understanding, or the steady support through life's challenges. It is these moments, though uncelebrated, that truly embody the essence of love.

Moreover, society often imposes a timeline on love, suggesting when it's appropriate to fall in love, marry, and even how quickly love should evolve. These unwritten rules add unnecessary pressure and can hasten the natural progression of relationships, leading to foundations built on sand rather than solid ground.

Love's portrayal as a state of constant happiness and fulfillment is a misconception that burdens many. True love encompasses a spectrum of emotions, including moments of doubt, pain, and conflict. Acknowledging this reality is pivotal in nurturing a resilient and genuine connection.

The expectation that love should be effortless perpetuates the myth that if one finds 'the one,' everything falls into place without struggle. In truth, love requires work, commitment, and the willingness to grow individually and as a couple. This misconceived notion of effortless love can deter individuals from investing the necessary effort, leading to the untimely demise of relationships.

Additionally, love's association with completeness, that one is incomplete without their partner undermines personal wholeness and independence. This notion romanticizes dependency and diminishes the individual's sense of self-worth outside the relationship.

Society celebrates the beginning of love – the infatuation stage – yet often disregards the deep, abiding love that matures over time. This oversight undervalues the beauty of love's evolution and the depth it reaches with time, misguiding individuals on what to expect from long-term partnerships.

As we peel away these layers of societal expectations, it becomes evident that love is not a one-size-fits-all experience. It's diverse, complex, and unique to every individual and relationship. Breaking free from the constraints of these societal norms allows for a more authentic and fulfilling exploration of love.

Challenging these stereotypes and expectations is not a sign of cynicism but of hope – hope for a more comprehensive understanding of love. It's an invitation to redefine love on more personal and realistic terms, setting the stage for relationships grounded in authenticity rather than fantasy.

Embracing love's true nature requires courage. It demands that we venture beyond the well-trodden path laid out by society to discover what love genuinely means to us as individuals. It's about finding harmony between the heart's feelings and the mind's choices, acknowledging that love is both a sentiment and a commitment to act.

The journey toward redefining love is both personal and collective. It begins with introspection and extends to conversations within our communities. By sharing our experiences and insights, we collectively weave a richer, more inclusive tapestry of love that acknowledges its multifaceted nature.

In this quest to understand love beyond societal expectations, we are not just seeking to enrich our lives but also to pave the way for future generations. A path where love is not confined by norms but is celebrated in its comprehensiveness and depth, cultivating relationships that are both fulfilling and sustainable.

Then, with open hearts and minds, let us embrace this journey towards a deeper understanding of love. Unshackling ourselves from the constraints of societal expectations, we can discover the boundless possibilities of love in its purest form, fostering connections deeply rooted in genuine understanding, prudence, and mutual growth.

The Philosophical Quest for Understanding Love As we glide from chapter to chapter, we embark on a journey into the soul's garden, exploring the essence of love. This quest is as ancient as philosophy, where thinkers have toiled to unlock the mysteries enshrouded in love's embrace. Love has always been a central theme in the pursuit of wisdom, for it profoundly challenges the mind and enriches the spirit.

But what is this mystery called love that philosophers have pondered over millennia? It's a question that seems to slip through the fingers of definitions, constantly transforming yet perpetually rooted in our human experience. Love, in its many forms, acts as a beacon guiding us through life's tumultuous seas, yet its essence remains elusive, compelling us to look deeper into our souls and the fabric of the universe.

Through the ages, philosophers have approached love from various angles. Some viewed it as a force of nature, as inevitable as the tide's ebb and flow, while others painted it as a divine flame, illuminating the darkness of mere existence. These explorations often reflected the proclivities of their times, a mirror to society's understanding and valuation of love.

The quest for understanding love isn't merely academic; it's a deeply personal pilgrimage. Each individual embarks on this journey, consciously or not, weaving through experiences that carve the contours of their understanding of love. It's a universal expedition, yet strikingly unique to every soul that breathes and loves.

One might argue that to grasp love philosophically, one must first distinguish its forms. The Greeks presented a blueprint with their concepts of Eros, Philia, Agape, and Storge—each a different manifestation of love's vast empire. This depiction prompts us to consider the nature of our affection, its source, and its aim. In doing so, it becomes apparent that love's essence cannot be confined to mere emotional states or duties; it encompasses a spectrum of human experience and spiritual yearning.

However, to reduce love to formulaic definitions or categories would be to miss an essential aspect of its nature. Love, in its purest form, transcends. It transcends language, logic, and even reason itself. Love is an experience felt in the depths of the soul, an art form that defies precise replication or explanation. It's both profoundly personal and immeasurably universal.

Philosophers have debated whether love is an inherent trait or a cultivated skill. Is it something we're born with, an ember waiting to be kindled, or is it a craft to be honed through the trials and triumphs of life? Perhaps it's a bit of both—a primal force that evolves with our willingness to nurture and understand it.

In pursuing love's meaning, there's a dance between the emotional and the rational, the subjective and the objective. This dance is where much of philosophy finds its tension and its beauty. It challenges us to embrace the complexities of love, question, and seek without necessarily arriving at a finite destination.

Love's philosophical quest is also a mirror to our values and beliefs. It reflects how we see ourselves, others, and the world. It's about connection and separation, about finding unity in diversity. In contemplating love, we also delve into notions of self, ethics, purpose, and the very essence of being.

Moreover, this quest instigates a confrontation with the paradoxes of love. It invites us to ponder why something infused with immense joy can also be a wellspring of profound sorrow. It forces us to wrestle with our vulnerabilities and strengths, highlighting love's power to heal and harm.

The philosophical exploration of love also beckons us towards the future. It challenges us to envision new paradigms of love that transcend traditional boundaries and expectations. This forward-looking perspective is about reimagining relationships and fostering a deeper sense of empathy and connection that could redefine society at large.

Yet, amid these philosophical musings, love remains an experiential truth. It's known more intimately in the hearts that feel it than in the texts that dissect it. This reality doesn't diminish the value of our philosophical quest; rather, it enriches it. It reminds us that love, in all its complexity and simplicity, is ultimately about connection—a thread linking heart to heart, soul to soul.

In pondering love, we're beckoning a journey with no definitive end. Each insight, each revelation leads to new questions, new mysteries. This endless quest might seem daunting, but it's therein that love reveals its true beauty. It's a journey that enriches our lives, relationships, and understanding of the world around us.

Thus, the philosophical quest for understanding love is more than an intellectual exercise; it's a vital, dynamic journey that touches the core of our being. It's an invitation to explore, to dream, and to love more deeply. In this exploration, we may discover that love, in its essence, is both a question and an answer—a mystery that, when embraced, illuminates the path to our most profound truths.

In essence, as we quest for understanding, let us remember: to philosophize about love is to participate in its dance, to contribute a verse in its eternal song. It's an adventure that calls for our whole being, inviting us to explore the depths of our soul and the expanses of the human spirit. This is the philosophical quest for understanding love—a journey without end, yet full of moments that define our very existence.

Definitions Across Culture and Time As we voyage through the myriad expressions and understandings of love across cultures and eras, we embark on a journey not just through geographical landscapes but through the very essence of human emotion and connection. The quest to define love has been as diverse as humanity itself, with each culture adding its unique hue to the spectrum of love.

In ancient Greece, love was dissected into various forms - Eros, Agape, Philia, and Storge. Eros, the passionate and intense form of love, contrasts sharply with Agape, the selfless, unconditional love. Philia speaks to the deep, platonic connections between friends, while Storge reflects the natural affection within families. These distinctions underscore the Greeks' deep investigation into the nuances of love, highlighting that love's essence cannot be confined to a single definition.

Traveling eastward, the concept of love in Hindu philosophy is encapsulated in the word *Prema*, which transcends the physical realm to reach the spiritual. It's a love that binds the soul, seeking unity and oneness not just with another being but with the universe and the divine. This view of love expands our understanding beyond the confines of the personal, inviting us to perceive love as an integral part of our spiritual journey.

In the lush landscapes of Africa, love finds expression in the practices and traditions that bind communities. Here, love is not just an emotion felt but an action performed, woven into the very fabric of society through acts of solidarity, communal support, and respect for the ancestral lineage. Love becomes a collective asset, shared and celebrated by all.

Jumping across the Atlantic to the pre-Columbian civilizations of the Americas, love was often intertwined with reverence for nature and cosmic forces. The Mayans, for example, viewed love as part of the balance of life, a personal and cosmic force connecting individuals to the larger mysteries of existence.

In contemporary Western societies, love has often been romanticized, sometimes to unrealistic proportions. The quest for a soulmate, the one true love, has permeated popular culture, shaping our expectations and experiences of love in profound ways. This view, while beautiful, sometimes skews our understanding of love's complexity and the work required to nurture and sustain it.

As we take a step back to view these varied perspectives in their entirety, it becomes apparent that love, in its essence, is a multifaceted gem. It adapts and changes not just with cultural shifts but with the personal evolution of each individual. Love is both universal and incredibly personal, a paradox that adds to its mystique and allure.

Yet, amidst this diversity, a common theme emerges: love is not merely an emotion to be felt but a force to be enacted. Whether it's the selfless devotion found in Agape, the communal bonds in African traditions, or the spiritual unity of Prema, love inspires action. It motivates us to transcend our limitations, serve, and give, highlighting the misconception that love is passive.

This realization invites us to reconsider our approach to love. Rather than viewing it as a feeling to be chased, we can embrace it as a guiding principle for our actions. Serving others, contributing to our communities, and choosing kindness and empathy become expressions of this profound force.

In this light, love becomes not just a part of our personal lives but a transformative power that can shape societies. Expanding our definitions of love to include these acts of service, we embrace a more comprehensive and action-oriented view of love. This perspective encourages us to build connections that transcend superficial boundaries, fostering deeper understanding and empathy among individuals and communities.

In conclusion, love, therefore, is an evolutionary force. As humanity progresses, so too does our understanding of love. What remains constant, however, is love's transformative power – its capacity to heal, to unite, and to inspire. This eternal aspect of love reminds us that irrespective of time or culture, love is the ultimate expression of our shared humanity.

Chapter 4:
Portrayals of Love in Literature and Media

The journey from the tangled roots of love's philosophical inquiries leads us naturally into the lush, vivid landscapes painted by literature and media. In this realm, love emerges not just as a feeling but as a living, breathing entity, ever subject to the beholder's eyes and the era's societal heartbeat. Literature, with its rich tapestry of words, has long served as a mirror, reflecting the evolving face of love, while media, in its visual splendor, casts shadows and light on love's modern-day interpretations. This chapter delves into how stories, poems, films, and songs sculpt our understanding of love—sometimes distorting it under the guise of grand romantic gestures, at other times elevating mundane moments to acts of profound significance. The portrayal of love in these forms challenges us to question: is love truly as we see it through these prisms, or have we been deceived into chasing after illusions crafted by masterful storytellers? As we traverse history and narratives, we uncover that the essence of love might lie in the simplicity of voluntarily and sacrificially serving another, a notion often glossed over by the dramatic flair of fictional accounts. This exploration beckons us to sift through layers of portrayal to find love's true core, encouraging us to redefine it beyond the confines of traditional depictions into a territory where love is as much about the quiet acts of giving as it is about the thunderous declarations of feeling.

Tracing Love in Classic Literature Within the maze of classic literature, we trace the contours of love, discovering its multitudes and mysteries. The quest to understand love's true essence through the prism of time-honored texts isn't merely academic—it's a journey into the heart of human experience.

In classic literature, love often emerges not as a singular emotion but as a complex amalgamation of feelings, actions, and sacrifices. Such narratives offer a rich tapestry from which we can draw insights into the nature of love—insights that illuminate love's endurance through the ages and its ability to adapt and thrive in myriad human conditions.

Consider, for a moment, the passionate, tumultuous love depicted in "Wuthering Heights." Emily Brontë's masterpiece doesn't merely capture the heart's tempests and probes love's darker sides. Here, love is a force of nature, wild and consuming—an echo of the human condition in its rawest form. Yet, at its core, it reveals love's capacity for deep, albeit destructive, connection.

On a different note, Jane Austen's "Pride and Prejudice" offers a sophisticated counterpoint. Austen deftly navigates the intricate social dances of her era to reveal love as a force for personal transformation and social cohesion. Through Elizabeth Bennet and Mr. Darcy's evolving relationship, love is shown as a journey of mutual understanding and respect. This evolution underscores love's potential to serve as a bridge between disparate worlds.

Shakespeare, the bard of love, provides perhaps the most diverse exploration of love's facets. From "Romeo and Juliet's" youthful, idealistic passion to "Hamlet's" complex filial love, Shakespeare's work is a testament to love's multifaceted nature. His works remind us that love can be both a source of great joy and profound tragedy, underscoring the delicate balance that love demands of the human heart.

Moving beyond the Western canon, "The Tale of Genji" by Murasaki Shikibu, written in early 11th century Japan, embodies love's ability to transcend time and culture. This intricate narrative, considered by many as the world's first novel, explores love's power, its transient beauty, and the pain of unfulfilled desire, offering a different perspective on the human condition.

Similarly, in "Les Misérables," Victor Hugo portrays love as a redemptive and transformative force amidst social unrest in 19th-century France. Through the lives of its characters, Hugo illustrates how love can drive change, both personal and societal, echoing the transformative power of love rooted in compassion and sacrifice.

These classics, each in their unique way, challenge us to consider whether love is about feelings alone. They present love as a complex interplay of emotions and actions that forge connections that can withstand the tests of time and circumstance.

What becomes evident through this exploration is the timeless nature of love's questions. Are love's trials unique to our time or universal across ages? Classic literature suggests that love has always been a multifaceted experience, shaped by the context of its time yet perennially challenging individuals to grow, adapt, and transcend their limitations.

This journey through classic literature thus acts as a mirror, reflecting back to us the timeless and evolving faces of love. It prompts us to question the shallow, often commercialized portrayals of love in modern media, urging us to delve deeper into love's essence—a quest that is both ancient and urgently contemporary.

By engaging with these texts, we not only honor the wisdom of the past but also enrich our own understanding. In doing so, we can begin to unravel some of the misconceptions that have clouded our perception of love, rediscovering its depth, its challenges, and its ultimate rewards.

As we traverse these landscapes, we find that love, in its purest form, often embodies a paradox. It is both feeling and action—emotion and service. To love is to feel deeply and to serve selflessly, sometimes in the very same breath. This duality lies at the heart of love's enduring mystery and its lasting appeal in our collective imagination.

Thus, tracing love in classic literature is more than an academic exercise; it is a journey into the heart of what it means to be human. It is an invitation to engage with love's complexities and to emerge with a more nuanced, perhaps even transformative, understanding of love itself.

In light of this exploration, we're left with a compelling invitation: to view love not just as a feeling to be cherished but as a call to action to be heeded. The stories we've inherited compel us to love more deeply, serve more faithfully, and walk the path of love with a keen awareness of its power to transform both ourselves and the world around us.

In conclusion, the classic literature's exploration of love calls us to a higher understanding of love, urging us to conceptualize it not merely as a feeling but as a profound force for good, capable of inspiring change, fostering connection, and nurturing the human spirit. As we navigate the complexities of love in our lives, let us draw wisdom from these timeless stories, allowing them to guide our hearts and actions.

Modern Media and the Illusions of Love In this age of digital enchantment, the portrayal of love in modern media often spins a web of illusion, painting pictures of passion, conflict, and resolution in colors more vibrant than the reality most of us recognize. This divergence between fantasy and truth has permeated our collective consciousness, subtly skewing our perceptions of what love is — and what it should be.

At the heart of these illusions lies the notion that love is a whirlwind of emotions, capable of overcoming any obstacle through the sheer force of feeling. We are fed stories of love at first sight, eternal devotion, and overcoming insurmountable hurdles through films, books, and songs. Yet, this romanticization glosses over the essence of love as an act of continuous sacrificial service, of voluntarily choosing the other daily despite the myriad challenges life throws our way.

Consider the popular narratives that dominate the screens and pages. They often conclude with the union of the lovers, as if to suggest that the culmination of love is in its realization, not in its sustenance. This leaves out the unwritten chapters that involve the mundane yet meaningful expressions of love — the shared chores, the compromises, the support during loss, and the encouragement in personal growth.

The influence of these narratives cannot be understated. They subtly implant expectations in our minds, expectations that real-life relationships can rarely live up to. When the initial fire of passion dims, as it naturally does, we are left wondering if something is amiss. Are we falling out of love, or have we, perhaps, been chasing an illusion?

What's more, the role of social media in shaping our ideas of love adds another layer of complexity. Platforms are flooded with snapshots of perfect moments, meticulously curated to portray an ideal that is often far from the lived reality. The visibility of these moments creates a perpetual comparison, a benchmark against which our relationships are measured and, more often than not, found wanting.

To untangle the web of illusions, we must begin with awareness. Acknowledging that the portrayals we consume are often far removed from the reality of love is a starting point. It allows us to question and critique rather than passively absorb these messages.

But awareness alone is not enough. It must be coupled with effort — the effort to redefine the depictions of love we see, to prioritize connection, commitment, and compassion over fleeting feelings of ecstasy. It's about embracing love as a verb, an action we choose daily, rather than a passive state of being.

In practice, this means fostering communication, practicing empathy, and putting in the work to understand and cherish our partners. It means placing intentional interest in little things, in the everyday acts that go unnoticed in the grand narratives of modern media.

This reinterpretation of love calls for a shift in perspective from the external to the internal. It invites us to turn away from the screens and look into the eyes of our loved ones, to see, to listen, to understand. In these genuine connections — imperfect and challenging as they may be — we find the true essence of love.

So, as we navigate the sea of images and stories that bombard us from every direction, let us anchor ourselves in the reality of love as it is lived. Let us cherish the quiet moments, the small gestures, and the simple acts of kindness that constitute the daily bread of love.

Ultimately, the journey towards understanding love in its most accurate form is personal and collective. It requires us to critically engage with the narratives we consume, to question and redefine them in the light of our own experiences and values. It's a call to action, an invitation to actively shape the discourse around love rather than passively accepting the illusions presented to us.

As we do so, we liberate ourselves from unrealistic expectations and pave the way for more authentic and fulfilling relationships. In recognizing and celebrating love in its many forms, we come closer to understanding its true nature — not as an idealized emotion but as a dynamic force for good, rooted in action, choice, and a deep commitment to the welfare of others.

Ultimately, love is not a storyline's grand gestures or climactic resolutions. It's the quiet, steadfast presence in our lives, the gentle hand guiding us through the storms, the light that illuminates the darkness. Moving beyond the illusions, we can appreciate love for what it truly is — a journey of growth, understanding, and service. As such, an inference could be drawn that, by definition, love is voluntary sacrificial service characterized by a mutually reciprocal commitment that is persistent, consistent, prolonged, and sustained in nature, ensuring the well-being of others is achieved and maintained.

Let this exploration of love in the modern media age serve not as an end but a beginning. The beginning of a deeper conversation about what love is, what it could be, and how we can collectively work towards a more authentic understanding of this most fundamental human experience.

Chapter 5:
Sonnets and Scriptures: A Comparative Analysis

In this journey through the landscapes of love, where whispers of the heart echo in timeless words, we delve into the realms of sonnets and scriptures to unravel the essence of love in its purest form. At the heart of our exploration lies a comparative analysis of Shakespeare's Sonnet 116 and the biblical 1 Corinthians 13, two profound pieces that, despite their different origins, converge on the essence of love. By comparing these timeless works, we uncover their universal truths, revealing that love's true nature transcends mere sentimentality to embody an unwavering force of constancy, resilience, and servitude. This chapter dares to peel away layers of misconception, shedding light on love not just as a fleeting emotion but as a sacred act of selflessness and dedication. Through this analysis, we embark on a transformative journey, encouraging us to embrace love's multifaceted dimensions—where serving becomes not just an obligation but the highest expression of love itself. Let's navigate these waters together, uncovering the richness of understanding love through the poetic elegance of sonnets and the divine wisdom of scriptures, illuminating a path toward embracing love in its most authentic form.

Compare Sonnet 116 and 1 Corinthians 13 In literature and scripture, few pieces have been as enduring and influential in our understanding of love as William Shakespeare's Sonnet 116 and the Apostle Paul's words in 1 Corinthians 13. Though emerging from vastly different contexts, cultures, and times, these texts converge in their exploration of love's true essence. This comparative analysis seeks not only to uncover the layers of meaning each work exudes but also to shed light on the universal truths of love that resonate through the ages.

The opening lines of Sonnet 116, "Let me not to the marriage of true minds/Admit impediments," introduce love as an unyielding force that transcends physical and temporal boundaries. Shakespeare's portrayal of love is romantic, marking it as an everlasting beacon undisturbed by the storms of reality. It's a declaration that true love does not change despite changing circumstances.

Similarly, 1 Corinthians 13 opens with a powerful assertion of love's supremacy, emphasizing that without love, one's actions and sacrifices are devoid of value. The Apostle Paul delineates love not through poetic imagery but by attributing to its characteristics: patience, kindness, devoid of envy, not boastful, and always hopeful. This passage roots love in moral and ethical behavior, showcasing it as the greatest virtue that stands above all else, including faith and hope.

Shakespeare's sonnet delves into love's capacity to withstand the test of time. "Love is not love/ Which alters when it alteration finds," he writes, advocating for a constant, unshakable love even as the loved ones themselves change. This perspective encapsulates love as an eternal truth, immune to the passage of time and external influences.

In contrast, Paul's discourse in 1 Corinthians 13 presents love as an action and choice rather than a mere feeling or state of being. His description implies that love is something one does, highlighting behaviors and actions that embody love. This portrayal suggests that love is dynamic actively lived, and expressed through our interactions and treatment of others.

While Shakespeare employs metaphor and imagery to encapsulate the grandeur of love, Paul uses a more direct and pragmatic approach.

This difference in style underscores their respective aims - Shakespeare's goal is to immortalize the ideal of love, and Paul's is to provide a guideline for living a life of love as dictated by Christian virtues.

One striking similarity between these texts is their acknowledgment of love's indomitability. For Shakespeare, love is an ever-fixed mark that "looks on tempests and is never shaken." Paul echoes this resilience in his assertion that love "bears all things, believes all things, hopes all things, endures all things." Both affirm love's capacity to endure, giving it a timeless and universal appeal.

However, a notable divergence lies in the ultimate purpose of these love portrayals. Shakespeare's sonnet is an ode to the steadfastness of romantic love, often interpreted as a defense against the criticisms and doubts of love's critics. On the other hand, Paul's text serves as a moral and ethical framework within the Christian faith, stressing love as the foundation of a virtuous life. It's a guide for conduct rather than an improvisation for a lover.

Moreover, Shakespeare's abstract depiction allows for a broader interpretation of love, potentially encompassing all forms of love, including friendship and kinship. Conversely, while primarily addressing agape - selfless, sacrificial, unconditional love - Paul's detailed description also underscores the practical aspects of how love should manifest in everyday human relationships.

Both texts conclude with affirmations of love's permanence. Sonnet 116 ends with a bold claim on love's enduring nature, challenging that if anyone can prove him wrong, his writings are lies, and no man has ever truly loved. Paul concludes by positioning love as the greatest among faith, hope, and love, thus cementing its importance in Christian virtues.

Why does this comparison matter? In our quest to understand love, we often look for it in the wrong places or define it in narrow terms. Sonnet 116 and 1 Corinthians 13 serve as timeless reminders that love, in its purest form, is much more than fleeting emotions or transient desires. It is patient, kind, enduring, and, above all, an act of will far beyond the grasp of time and decay.

Embracing the lessons from these texts can inspire a deeper comprehension and appreciation of love in our lives. They teach us that love's true power lies not in grand gestures or eloquent words but in everyday acts of kindness, understanding, and perseverance.

In a world that often misconstrues love with superficiality and instant gratification, Sonnet 116 and 1 Corinthians 13 invite us to reflect on the essence of genuine love. They encourage us to love bravely and steadfastly in the face of challenges and beyond the allure of idealized notions.

Ultimately, this comparative analysis enlightens us about these historical texts and invites us to introspect on the nature of love in our lives. It challenges us to question: Is our understanding of love serving us—or are we serving love? Are we embodying the virtues of patience, kindness, and endurance that these texts beautifully champion?

By integrating the wisdom from Sonnet 116 and 1 Corinthians 13 into our lives, we can strive towards a higher, more fulfilling love that transcends the confines of time and space, is rooted in actions, and is upheld by an unwavering commitment to its true essence.

Interpreting Love Through Shakespeare and the Bible As we delve into the complexities and sublimities of love, it becomes evident that this emotion, this indispensable facet of human experience, defies simplistic definitions. In our quest to grasp its essence, we turn to two of the most profound sources in literature and religious scripture: the sonnets of William Shakespeare and the verses of the Bible. Each, in its unique way, offers a lens through which the multifaceted nature of love can be interpreted and understood.

At first glance, one might question what the Elizabethan playwright and the sacred scriptures have in common. Yet, upon closer examination, it becomes clear that both grapple with the conception of love in ways that transcend the boundaries of time and culture. With their eloquent expressions of affection, passion, and longing, Shakespeare's sonnets complement the Bible's teachings on love's spiritual and moral dimensions.

For instance, Shakespeare's Sonnet 116 proclaims, "Love is not love which alters when it alteration finds." Here, Shakespeare speaks to the steadfastness of true love, an idea that echoes throughout the pages of the Bible, especially in 1 Corinthians 13:7, which states, "Love bears all things, believes all things, hopes all things, endures all things." Though emerging from vastly different contexts, both texts converge on the notion that love is unwavering and enduring in its purest form.

This convergence highlights a fundamental misconception about love: it is not merely a fleeting emotion, subject to the whims of circumstance. Instead, both Shakespeare and the Bible invite us to view love as a steadfast commitment, a choice to remain constant irrespective of the inevitability of life's challenges.

Moreover, the emphasis on love as an action rather than merely a feeling becomes apparent when examining these texts further. The Bible, particularly in the New Testament, conceptualizes love as an active, selfless giving of oneself to others. It posits love as the highest commandment, encompassing patience, kindness, and humility. "Love your neighbor as yourself," it commands, urging us to extend our love beyond the confines of our personal desires and affections.

Shakespeare also captures the essence of love's selflessness in his portrayals of love. His sonnets speak of love as a force that transcends the personal, touching on themes of sacrifice and enduring loyalty. In his depiction, love is not merely about possession or the satisfaction of desire but about the willingness to put another's needs and well-being above one's own.

This brings us to the heart of our exploration: the realization that love is not merely about feelings. To love is to act with kindness and consideration, to support and uplift, to endure and forgive. Both Shakespeare's sonnets and the biblical scriptures lead us to this understanding, coaxing us to look beyond the surface-level emotions and delve into the deeper commitments that love entails.

Through their exploration of love, both sources also reveal that love is inherently tied to growth and transformation. As we love, we are called to rise above our basest instincts and embrace a higher standard of behavior and being. This process is not without its challenges, requiring self-examination, humility, and the courage to change.

It's essential, then, to acknowledge that love's path is not always smooth. Both Shakespeare and the Bible do not shy away from portraying the difficulties that come with loving deeply. They show us that love's strength is not just in its joys but in its capacity to endure pain, misunderstandings, grief, and loss.

In our modern context, where love is often idealized and romanticized, the insights from Shakespeare's sonnets and the Bible are particularly poignant. They remind us that love encompasses much more than passion and emotion. It is a guiding principle for living, encouraging us to embrace empathy, compassion, and altruism.

Thus, interpreting love through the lens of Shakespeare and the Bible enables us to see beyond the surface-level portrayals of love that dominate popular culture. It challenges us to redefine love in terms of commitment, service, and transformation, encouraging us to adopt a more profound and fulfilling approach to our relationships.

In conclusion, as we reflect on the teachings of these two monumental sources, let us strive to embody the true essence of love in our daily lives. Let us commit to being patient, kind, and selfless, to bearing and enduring all things in love. In doing so, we not only enrich our individual lives but also contribute to creating a world where love prevails in its most genuine and transformative form.

May this exploration of love through Shakespeare's sonnets and the Bible inspire us to look beyond the transient and the superficial. May it encourage us to forge connections rooted in the enduring and the eternal, in the understanding that love, in its essence, is not just about how we feel but how we serve.

Let this understanding of love inform our relationships and guide us in all our interactions. In interpreting love as Shakespeare and the Bible teach us, we find a blueprint for a life lived with depth, purpose, and a heart opened to its transformative power.

Chapter 6:
The Cultural Evolution of Love

In the unwavering journey from the rugged terrains of antiquity to the sleek highways of contemporary society, love has consistently proven to be the most malleable of sentiments, shape-shifting through ages, adapting to cultural paradigms, and reflecting the societal ethos of every age. The concept of love has evolved dramatically from being a strategic alliance between families in ancient societies to a quest for personal happiness and fulfillment in modern times. This transformation has not been straightforward or uniform across cultures; it has been a vibrant mosaic, rich with diverse interpretations and practices. As we traverse from the past to the present, it becomes apparent that love, in its essence, has always been a reflection of human needs and societal structures. However, despite its evolving facade, the core of love remains a quest for connection, understanding, and acceptance. This chapter delves into the heart of how cultures across time have painted love, from the chivalric love in medieval times, the passionate, often tragic love of the Romantic era, to today's digital age love intertwined with technology. It is a journey through time, exploring how the expression of love has changed, yet how it continues to be the eternal thread woven into the fabric of human existence, driving us toward the elusive yet universal quest for belonging and acceptance. The cultural evolution of love is not just a history of changing norms but a mirror reflecting our collective journey through time, challenging us to ponder what love truly means in our own lives.

Love in Antiquity As we venture back in time to explore the ancient perceptions of love, we find ourselves in a world where the concepts and expressions of love were as vast and diverse as the civilizations themselves. The ancients seemed to understand love deeply, encapsulating its multifaceted nature through myths, texts, and rituals. By examining their beliefs and practices, we might unravel misconceptions of love and discover its essence—is it merely a feeling, or is it deeply rooted in serving?

In ancient Egypt, love was often depicted as a powerful force that could unite the gods with mortals. Their mythology is laced with romantic love tales emphasizing devotion and sacrifice. For instance, the story of Isis and Osiris teaches us the power of love to transcend even death. Isis's unwavering love for Osiris motivates her to reassemble his scattered body. Here, love transforms into actions of service, a theme that resonates through centuries.

Greek civilization categorized love, articulating it through various types—Eros, Philia, Agape, and Storge. Each type reflected a unique aspect of love, from the passionate desire and intimacy of Eros to the selfless and giving nature of Agape. The Greeks contemplated love's complexities, encouraging a balanced perspective that acknowledged love's emotional and service-oriented dimensions.

Meanwhile, in Rome, the poet Ovid's "Ars Amatoria" suggests a more practical approach to love, intertwining it with strategy and technique. However, beneath this surface, there's a subtle acknowledgment of love's deeper essence, suggesting that true love involves devotion and a readiness to act on behalf of the loved one. It is in these acts of service, perhaps, that love's true nature is revealed.

The ancient Indian epic, the Mahabharata, reflects on love through stories of duty, courage, and sacrifice. Here, love is seen as a duty bound by Dharma (righteousness). The characters' journeys underscore love's multifaceted nature, where passionate love (Kama) coexists with dutiful action. This integration suggests love cannot be confined to mere feelings; it flourishes in selfless acts and loyalty.

Turning to ancient China, the philosophy of Confucianism emphasizes Ren (benevolence or humaneness) as a fundamental aspect of love. Confucian texts urge followers to express love through ethical actions and moral conduct towards others, proposing that true love is manifested in the care for the well-being of another, highlighting love's intrinsic connection to service.

When considering love in antiquity, one cannot overlook the profound poetic contributions of the Sufi mystics in the Islamic Golden Age. Poets like Rumi and Hafiz explored love as a pathway to the divine, suggesting that earthly love mirrors the divine. Here, love becomes an act of devotion, not only to the beloved but to the love itself as an exalted state of being.

In examining these ancient perspectives, it becomes evident that love, in its essence, was seldom confined to mere emotional expressions. Instead, it was understood through actions, dedication, and conscious choice to serve the one you love. This universal theme challenges contemporary views that often prioritize emotional highs, suggesting that true love encompasses a broader, more profound spectrum of experiences.

This exploration into the past raises pertinent questions about today's understanding of love. In pursuing romantic idealizations, have we overlooked the fundamental essence of love our ancestors seemingly understood so well? The notion that love extends beyond feelings into action and service offers a grounded, perhaps more sustainable perspective on love.

As we reflect on love's portrayal through ancient myths, texts, and philosophies, we find a consistent thread—the undeniable link between love and acts of service. Whether through the devotion of Isis, the ethical conduct prescribed by Confucius, or the selfless love depicted in the Mahabharata, ancient civilizations recognized that love is as much about giving as it is about feeling.

This historical perspective empowers us to reconsider our individual perspectives on love. It prompts us to ask ourselves whether our expressions of love are as deep and multifaceted as those that have stood the test of time. In doing so, we're encouraged to cultivate a love that feels profoundly and acts generously.

As we journey through life, let us carry with us the wisdom of the ancients. Let love be more than an emotion felt but a service rendered. Love reveals its truest form in every act of kindness, in every sacrifice made, and in every deed done for the well-being of another.

Thus, Love in Antiquity is a compelling reminder of love's timeless essence. It challenges us to expand our understanding of love, embrace its complexities, and express it in ways that transcend the temporary euphoria.

In conclusion, the ancients teach us that love, in its purest form, intertwines feeling with serving. By embracing both aspects, we encounter a more complete, more satisfying expression of love—one that nourishes ourselves and the world around us. As we reflect on these ancient teachings, let love be both a splendid feeling we cherish and a noble voluntary sacrificial service we joyfully perform.

Contemporary Views on Love and Relationships The landscape of love and relationships has profoundly transformed in the modern era. Today, we are bombarded with varied perceptions of love and how it should manifest in our connections.

Recently, the advent of technology and the internet has radically reshaped our interactions, thus influencing contemporary views on love. These technologies foster connections across vast distances and present a paradox. On the one hand, they enable us to maintain relationships across miles and time zones; on the other, they sometimes reduce our interactions to superficial exchanges, leaving some to ponder the depth and authenticity of connections forged in digital realms.

It's also worth noting how self-love has gained prominence in public discourse. Gone are the days when self-sacrifice was the ultimate proof of love. Currently, understanding and nurturing oneself is often considered the first step toward forming healthy and fulfilling relationships with others.

Yet, with these new realities, there's an undercurrent of skepticism. Some argue that the transient nature of modern relationships—fueled by dating apps and social media—might be eroding the foundational elements of deep, enduring love. They worry that the ease of forming connections could make them disposable, with less willingness to work through challenges.

Still, others celebrate the freedom and flexibility that contemporary relationships offer. They see the ability to enter and exit relationships as needed as a form of empowerment, allowing individuals to find what truly works for them without societal pressure to conform to traditional norms.

Moreover, the emphasis on communication has never been more pronounced. In an age where misunderstandings are but a text message away, the importance of clear, honest, and open communication is continually highlighted as the bedrock of solid relationships. This aligns with a growing understanding that love is not just about grand gestures but also daily acts of kindness, respect, and empathetic listening.

Amid these shifting paradigms, the challenge many face is finding a balance between independence and connection. There's a fine line between healthy self-love and isolation, between flexibility in relationships and commitment phobia. Navigating these complexities requires introspection, understanding, and a willingness to learn and adapt.

Furthermore, the resurgence of interest in ancient philosophies and practices related to love suggests a collective yearning for depth and meaning. Meditation, mindfulness, and personal growth are increasingly considered integral to cultivating love that transcends infatuation's emotional highs and lows.

The debate on whether love is more about feeling or serving continues to provoke thought. With society's growing acknowledgment of the impermanence of emotions, there's a rising appreciation for love as an action. In this context, serving is understood not as a harmful act but as a powerful expression of love that enriches both the giver and the receiver.

In the quest to untangle love's essence, blending old wisdom and new insights offers a promising path forward. It's a journey of recognizing love's diverse expressions while seeking a common thread that unites them all—compassion. Whether it's romantic love, familial bonds, friendships, or self-love, the emphasis on genuine care and understanding underscores contemporary views on relationships.

This exploration is not without its challenges, yet it's precisely through encountering and overcoming these obstacles that love's full spectrum is revealed. The modern narrative of love and relationships, with all its complexities and nuances, encourages us to embrace vulnerability, practice empathy, and celebrate the connections that bring meaning to our lives.

In conclusion, the contemporary views on love and relationships are a tapestry woven from threads of tradition and innovation. As we navigate this intricate landscape, let us remember that at the heart of love—past, present, and future—is the pursuit of genuine connection and shared growth. It is in this space that the true magic of love resides, endlessly adapting yet forever rooted in the timeless virtues of compassion, understanding, and respect.

Chapter 7:
The Misconceptions and Idealizations of Love

In the journey to uncover the essence of love, it's imperative we confront the myriad misconceptions and idealizations that have distorted its true nature. Far beyond the high drama and the swept-off-feet moments celebrated in movies and novels, love's reality is often painted with subtler, deeper shades. Society, with its glossy, airbrushed portrayals, sells us an image of love that's all about fiery passion and flawless companionship, yet this neglects the very foundation of what love entails. It's about showing up, about the quiet acts of care and the steady hand of support through life's tumult. The mornings spent together in silence, the comforting presence amid uncertainty and the mutual respect underpin every gesture. The real question we must ask ourselves isn't whether love feels good, but rather, does it serve? Does it uplift? Does it contribute to our growth and the well-being of others? This chapter aims to peel back the layers of fantasy to reveal the core of love's proper form: a force that's less about possession and more about liberation, less about ceaseless happiness, and more about the strength to face life's challenges together. In doing so, we can begin to disentangle the myths from realities, shifting our perceptions from what society says love should be to understanding the profound simplicity of what it actually is. Only then can we embrace love in its entirety, free from the idealizations that bind us to expectations and open to the boundless possibilities that genuine connection brings?

What Does Society Say about love? In the vast tapestry of human experience, the societal narrative surrounding love has been both a guiding light and a source of confusion. Our collective consciousness, fed by myriad influences, often dictates how we perceive love and how we pursue and practice it.

In modern times, society predominantly romanticizes love. As we are frequently told, love is the ultimate emotion, a force so profound that it can overcome any obstacle. This portrayal, while enchanting, can sometimes paint an incomplete picture, leaving many to chase an ideal without fully understanding the breadth and depth of genuine connection.

Consider for a moment the way love is presented in popular media. Films, novels, and songs champion the fiery, all-consuming infatuation phase, suggesting that such intensity is the hallmark of true love. Yet, this is a single layer, a mere beginning to the complex journey of shared lives. Real love, as those who have weathered the trials and tribulations of long-term relationships know, involves much more than initial chemistry. It requires patience, understanding, and a willingness to navigate the mundane alongside the magnificent.

Society often speaks of love in terms of completion, suggesting that finding our "other half" is the key to our wholeness. This narrative, while comforting, can inadvertently propagate the myth of the missing piece. It leads to a pursuit where individuals seek fulfillment outside themselves, neglecting the crucial journey towards self-awareness and self-love that ultimately enhances one's ability to love and be loved effectively.

The pressures of societal expectations regarding love are immense. Couples are often judged by their ability to adhere to conventional milestones – meeting, dating, marriage, and children – in a prescribed sequence. Yet, love's true essence cannot be so neatly categorized. Each relationship is a unique voyage, and what works for one pair may not suit another. The societal impulse to conform can stifle the authentic expression of love, squeezing it into a one-size-fits-all box.

Amidst this backdrop of evolving societal norms, the pressure to navigate love 'correctly' can be overwhelming. Young lovers are inundated with conflicting advice: be independent but not too distant; be passionate but not overly emotional. It's a balancing act where the rules seem to change with the wind, making the path to understanding love a challenging but rewarding endeavor.

The societal narrative is also heavily influenced by the commercialization of love. Holidays like Valentine's Day amplify notions of romantic love, often equating its expression with material gifts. This commodification can diminish the authenticity of love's expression, suggesting a transactional nature to emotions that are inherently immeasurable.

Moreover, the digital age has transformed the landscape of love. Social media platforms, offering glimpses into the relationships of others, can set unrealistic expectations. The curated portrayal of love online often excludes the struggles and conflicts integral to any relationship, leading some to question the validity of their emotions when faced with the messiness of real life.

However, a growing counter-narrative seeks to reclaim love from the clutches of idealization and commercialization. Advocates for a more grounded understanding of love emphasize its everyday expressions—acts of kindness, affirming words of support, and the quiet presence in times of need. This movement points to the actions behind the words, the serving aspect of love that sustains connections over time.

In essence, society's interpretation of love is dynamic, a shifting amalgam of ideals, beliefs, and emerging understandings. While the messages we receive about love can sometimes lead us astray, they also prompt us to question and, ultimately, define for ourselves what love means. Though fraught with challenges, this quest is also rich with opportunities for growth and deepening connections.

It behooves us to approach love with curiosity rather than certainty. By questioning societal prescriptions of love, we open ourselves to discovering its true essence. Love, in its purest form, isn't something to be achieved or displayed but rather a path to walk, a practice to deepen, and a value to embody.

Then, guided by the wisdom gleaned from our collective experiences, let us forge a path toward a love that is inclusive, compassionate, and reflective of the tapestry of human connection. In doing so, we honor not just the idea of love but its transformative potential in our lives and the world at large.

In conclusion, society says many things about love, but not all of them are complete or entirely helpful. Our task is not to passively accept these narratives but to engage with them critically, paving the way for a more holistic and comprehensive understanding of love. As we navigate this complex terrain, let us be both students and teachers, eager to learn from love's many guises and willing to share the insights our journeys afford us.

Disentangling Myths from Realities As we delve into the romantic notions that have been built around love, it's pivotal that we steer our ship through the fog of myths and dock at the harbor of realities. Often, love is painted in hues too vibrant, masking the actual colors that, though less vivid, are far more profound. This journey is about peeling off the layers of misconceptions and rediscovering love's authentic essence.

In our quest, we confront a rather prominent myth: the idea that love is purely a feeling. This myth whispers to us through cinema screens and the pages of novels, suggesting that love, in its proper form, is a whirlwind of emotion, always passionate and overwhelmingly consuming. Yet, as we sift through the grains of reality, we unearth a different truth. Love is as much a verb as it is a noun; it's an active choice, a series of actions and commitments beyond just the initial surge of feeling. Love is serving, enduring, and evolving.

Another widespread misconception is that love should be effortless, a smoothly paved road without bumps or turns. This fantasy can lead to disillusionment when the inevitable challenges of life emerge. Real love is about navigation, not avoidance. It requires effort, compromise, and growth. It's about facing the storms together and coming out stronger, not sailing only on sunny days.

It's also commonly believed that love can only be true if it is all-consuming, to the point where lovers lose themselves in each other. However, this can be a dangerous narrative, leading many to forsake their individuality in pursuing a romantic ideal. What's crucial to understand is that true love fosters independence and individual growth, understanding that two wholes make a stronger bond than two halves ever could.

The myth of 'the one' also merits address. While the idea of a sole soulmate for each person is romantic, it can be limiting and unrealistic. Love is not about finding the perfect person but seeing an imperfect person perfectly. It's about the deliberate choice to love someone in spite of, and sometimes because of, their flaws.

In disentangling these myths, we find love's realities are more grounded. Love is patient; it's kind and doesn't come with a condition tag. It thrives on mutual respect, understanding, and the willingness to work through differences. It's about building a foundation that withstands the wear and tear of time.

Furthermore, the modern idealization of constant happiness in love sets an unachievable standard. Real love encompasses a range of emotions, including moments of disappointment, frustration, and sorrow. It's not about perpetual bliss but sharing and overcoming life's myriad experiences together.

Another myth is that love is always fair and equal. However, the scales of give and take can fluctuate, and that's okay. There will be times when one partner needs to provide more and times when it's the other way around. The balance isn't always perfect, but love means being there, contributing what's needed when needed and within the proper measure, without keeping score.

It's also essential to debunk the myth that love means never arguing or disagreeing. In reality, conflict is a natural part of any relationship. It's not the absence of arguments that define the strength of a bond but the ability to resolve them respectfully and constructively.

The idea that love is all you need is another romantic notion that, while pleasing to the ear, is far from practical. Love is crucial, but for a relationship to thrive, it requires more—trust, respect, communication, and shared values. These elements and love build the infrastructure of a lasting relationship.

Moreover, societal standards often insinuate that love has an age, implying that it blossoms in youth and fades with time. This myth fails to acknowledge that love, in its essence, is ageless. It can spark at any stage of life and grow deeper with the passing of years, defying the limits of time.

Let's also dispel the myth that love makes everything easy. While love can be a source of strength and motivation, it doesn't erase life's challenges. Instead, it equips us to face them, offering a hand to hold during the battles we cannot fight alone.

Another misconception is that love is always serene and calm. While peace is a component of deep love, authentic connections are also fiery, dynamic, and sometimes tumultuous. Love encompasses a spectrum of experiences and emotions, from tranquility to tempests, each formative in its own right.

In recognizing that love is not the absence of difficulties but the presence of a bond that endures through them, we embrace a more realistic and enriching perspective. This view doesn't diminish love's magic but enriches it, grounding it in actions and choices that foster a deeper, more resilient connection.

Thus, in disentangling myths from realities, we don't dismantle the beauty of love; we refine it. We learn that love, in its most accurate form, isn't about living up to an idealized notion but cherishing and nurturing the real, flawed, and incredible journey of two souls choosing to walk together. And it is in this choice, this daily act of love, that we find its deepest meaning and most enduring magic.

Chapter 8:
Self-Love and Narcissism: An In-Depth Look

As the preceding chapters have paved the rigorous journey into the heart of love's multitude of expressions, we now scrutinize the fine line that demarcates self-love from the shadow it casts – narcissism. This chapter delves into this discourse, unwrapping the layers that differentiate a healthy self-regard from the trappings of an inflated ego. The wisdom to discern self-love's intimate tones, resonant with the care for one's well-being and growth, can often be muddied by society's glorification of self above all. In stark contrast to the shouty parade of narcissism, genuine self-love whispers a subtle yet persistent affirmation of one's value without tipping the scales toward the extremities of self-absorption. The journey here is about balancing on the tightrope of recognizing one's worth, not obscuring the humanity and needs of others—an authentic test of wisdom in the pursuit of love.

The Distinctions Between Selfish and Self-Love

In the restless journey towards understanding love, we tread a path littered with misconceptions and blurred lines, particularly in discerning self-love from selfishness. The distinction holds the key to perceiving and truly apprehending love's essence. Self-love and selfishness often masquerade as synonyms in the theater of society's varying scripts, yet they're inherently divergent. Self-love is a source; it is the wellspring from which the ability to love others flows abundantly and without the fear of depletion. It's not merely accepting who you are but nurturing your growth and well-being with the same tenderness you would offer to someone you hold dear.

Selfishness, on the other hand, entrenches the heart in isolation. It is a closed door, a one-way street that leads back to oneself with little regard for the navigation of others. To be selfish is to act with an excessive concern for one's advantage, pleasure, or welfare, disregarding, or even at the expense of, the welfare of others. Despite this stark difference, the two concepts are often confounded as they cross paths within human action and motivation.

Understanding this distinction begins with recognizing that self-love is reflective and generative. When you embrace self-love, you engage in introspection that results not in narcissism but in a profound realization of your worth – a recognition that does not inflate your ego but humbles you with gratitude for your existence. This form of love is foundational. It constructs a fortress of well-being and confidence from which you can venture forth to love others without losing yourself in them.

One of the greatest follies is the erroneous belief that taking time for oneself equates to selfishness. In the pilgrimage to understanding self-love, it's paramount to grasp that prioritizing your needs does not necessarily subtract from someone else's. True self-love equips you to meet others at the zenith of their needs without draining your reserves. It is knowing when to say 'no,' not out of spite or disregard but of the realization that overextension can lead to a diminished capacity to provide meaningful support to others.

Selfishness stagnates; it curbs learning and understanding as the selfish individual often refuses to see beyond their horizon. It breeds resentment and a fortress of solitude constructed with bricks of insecurity, behind which lies the dread of vulnerability. Selfish acts are often driven by fear – a fear of scarcity, a fear of not being enough, and a fear of not having enough. It is a misguided attempt to hoard love without realizing that true love, much like light, cannot be lessened by being shared.

Embracing self-love generates a ripple effect; it is contagious in its purest form. When you practice self-love, you set a standard for how you treat yourself and how you expect to be treated by others. This precedent affects how you engage in relationships and dictates the kind of love you will accept. Self-love, therefore, is a daily victory that involves the active decision to treat yourself with kindness, patience, and respect. It invites a life lived intentionally and richly, steeped in the value you attribute to your life.

Consider self-love as an embodiment of balance. It is the equilibrium in tending to your garden so that you may appreciate the beauty in someone else's without the envy that withers both. It is a nurturing process that requires diligence and the conscious understanding that self-care is not an act of rebellion but an act of survival, and beyond survival, it is the essence of thriving.

Achieving a distinction in love means learning when commitment to the self crosses the barrier into disregard for others. The application of wisdom in this realm becomes paramount. There exists a fine line whereby self-care must not evolve into a blind pursuit of self-interest, whereby being protective of one's energy does not morph into the relentless pursuit of one's gains. Here lies the process of discerning the heart's true intentions behind each act of supposed love.

The alignment of our intentions with actions reveals the nature of our hearts. Loving ourselves provides a template for interacting in the broader human emotion and connection spectrum. How we cherish our being forms the foundation of how we approach love in its multifaceted expressions. Our internal dialogues pave the pathways for our external stories. It's essential, then, to compose a narrative that extols self-worth without scripting the downfall of others.

Selfishness, clothed in hubris and pride, neither admits fault nor recognizes the weight of its footprints. To wield love selfishly is to control and to bind, reducing the vast expanse of love to strings upon which others might be pulled and manipulated. This is not the journey of love that seeks the well-being of all but rather the orchestration of circumstances that favor one. The selfish heart loves conditionally, constantly scanning the horizon for what it might glean rather than what it might give.

To exist within the spectrum of self-love means to stand in one's truth without casting shadows upon another. The cultivation of self-love engages one in a practice that is restorative, not retributive. When love for the self does not cast blame or sow seeds of judgment, it flowers into an open field where love for others can prosper. True self-love is then an invitation, a beacon that signals to those around us that love's nature is expansive, its territory uncharted and open for exploration together.

As we delve deeper into the nuances of love's character, we must find solace in the assurance that the love we instill within ourselves is not a reservoir running dry but a channel continuously replenished. From such a boundless spring, we can pour love in myriad directions without fear of emptiness.

Therefore, understanding love cannot be complete without the testimony of self-love and selflessness, each carrying its distinctive weight and significance. To love oneself truly is to have unraveled the myth that love is a finite commodity, discovering instead that it manifests most purely when given freely – starting with oneself and emanating outward.

In essence, self-love is an art – a meticulously crafted symphony that resonates with the tones of self-compassion, self-respect, and the unwavering understanding that to love oneself is a prerequisite to loving others wholesomely. To distinguish between self-love and selfishness is to discern between that which limits and that which liberates, granting us the perspective to embody love's true character and see it bloom in all its glory.

Choosing Health over Ego As we delve deeper into our exploration of love and its multifaceted existence, we must address a potent force that often stands as a barrier to authentic connections: the ego. In the dance of love, ego is the partner that steps on our toes, insisting on leading, when in truth, the rhythm calls for a harmonious duet. Embarking on this path, we must first disempower the tendencies that serve the ego to pave the way for a healthier self-love that resonates with the true essence of love.

Within the confines of the ego, love is often mistaken for ownership and control. This deception is a precarious slope, as the ego can shroud our perception in a veil of misguided love, where possessiveness masquerades as care. Consider the perennial tale of unrequited love, where one may persist despite disinterest from the other party. Here, the ego insists, 'If I can't have them, no one else will,' rather than stepping aside to honor the other's free will.

Love, in its purest state, is an exercise in humility and surrender. A willingness to diminish the ego allows for the flourishing of empathy, which fosters a love rooted in understanding and acceptance. When we choose to set aside our egotistical desires, we make room for the authentic growth of our relationships. This act is not one of defeat but of courage—a testament to our strength and commitment to true health and well-being.

The journey towards choosing health over ego begins with awareness. Recognizing the moments when our ego flares up in jealousy, vanity, or dominance provides us with the opportunity for introspection. Why do these feelings arise? From where do they stem? More often than not, they result from insecurities within ourselves that reflect in our relationships as demands for validation and assurance.

Self-love is the beacon that guides us through the shadow of the ego. Not to be confused with narcissism, which is self-love's impostor, genuine self-love nurtures our self-esteem without casting others to the margins. It's about giving ourselves the respect and care we often seek from others—reaffirming our worthiness of love from a wellspring of internal abundance.

Intrinsic self-worth alleviates the pressure on relationships to validate us constantly. When we know our value, we release our partners from the burden of propping up our self-image. This liberates both parties to love freely without the limitations that ego-driven entanglements often impose. Relationships become less about what one can take and more about what one can share.

Forgiveness plays a key role when we falter on our path, as we inevitably will. The ego resents and hoards grievances, yet proper health is found in letting go. Forgiveness is the salve that heals ego-inflicted wounds, allowing us to move forward unburdened by past disputes. Through forgiveness, we realize that holding onto anger serves no one—least of all ourselves.

Communication is another essential aspect of favoring health over ego. Expressing needs and desires transparently, without the façade of pride or pretense, fortifies bonds. When we communicate sincerely, we invite our loved ones to see us as we are, building a foundation of trust and respect that the ego's games would otherwise undermine.

Choosing health over ego also means embracing vulnerability. The ego fights vulnerability, viewing it as a weakness, but it is a profound strength in love. To be vulnerable is to be open to the full spectrum of experiences that relationships offer, including the risks of pain and disappointment. Nevertheless, we cultivate the most profound intimacy in this space, sharing joy, fears, and uncertainties.

Letting go of ego-based expectations frees us from the tyranny of perfect love—an ideal that exists only in fantasy. We learn to appreciate love's ebb and flow, imperfections, and transient nature. This acceptance is not resignation but an embrace of the reality that love is a living, evolving entity, not a static icon to be worshipped.

Choosing health over ego involves the courage to face one's shadows, engage with our less flattering traits, and address them head-on. It is a commitment to self-improvement and emotional intelligence, recognizing that the true enemy of love is not outside forces but the battles we wage within.

Consider the dynamics between independence and interdependence in relationships. The ego often clings to an exaggerated sense of freedom to avoid vulnerability. Yet, choosing health implies understanding the beauty of interdependence, where both partners can lean on each other, providing mutual support without forfeiting their individuality.

Ultimately, pursuing a healthy self-love that quells the ego is an act of bravery. It is a journey that is often less traveled, marked by profound introspection and the dismantling of barriers that preclude us from experiencing the fullness of love. When we opt for health, we're not just nurturing our relationships with others, but we're also honoring our sacred relationship with our creator.

This conquest over the ego reveals the essence of serving in love. The majesty of love reveals itself not in the towering proclamations or grand gestures but in the quiet, steadfast acts that place the well-being of others at the heart of our intentions. This is the fertile ground in which love thrives, blossoming into a bond that is both enduring and tender.

Therefore, when discussing health over ego, we advocate for a paradigm shift that places service, empathy, and authenticity above the ego's selfishness. Here, the misconceptions of love are dispelled, shining light on the truth that serving is not subservience but the highest form of love—a love that seeks the joy and welfare of others as its own. In the triumph of health over ego, we find love in its most genuine and liberating form.

Chapter 9:
Compassionate Love: Altruism and Empathy

In the tapestry of human experience, love is often displayed in rich, variegated threads but none so vibrant and healing as the hues of compassionate love. In this pure expression, we find the essence of altruism and empathy, extending beyond mere emotion into sacrificial service. Here, love is not trapped by self-gain trappings; instead, it reaches out in quiet anonymity, seeking to illuminate the shadowed places in others' lives. This chapter delves into the heart's capacity to transcend its needs, transforming empathy into catalysts for action and nurturing the charitable impulse that lies dormant within us. In understanding that love's accurate measure is in its giving, without expectation or design, we touch upon the profound ability within ourselves to effect change in the world one compassionate act at a time. Embrace this journey into the texture of compassion, where love does not stand still but moves inexorably towards the soul with an open hand, touching lives and, in resonance, our most profound humanity.

Scientific Perspectives on Compassionate Love As we delve into the intricacies of compassionate love, the scientific lens offers a shimmering clarity. You see, compassionate love is not just a vague/unattainable concept floating in the terrain of poetic discourse; it is deeply rooted in empirical evidence and neurobiological processes that reveal its profound significance in human connectivity. How does science dissect this compelling aspect of the heart's endeavors?

Neuroscientists have mapped areas of the brain that light up when individuals engage in charitable acts, a key component of compassionate love. The prefrontal cortex, associated with complex cognitive behavior and decision-making, and the anterior insula, linked to consciousness and emotion, show increased activity when one expresses compassion. This suggests a biological foundation, indicating that compassionate love is an innate and critical feature of humanity's social framework.

Studies in psychology have revealed that compassionate love can bolster mental health. When individuals show compassion, they often experience a decrease in stress-related responses and an increase in positive emotions. This, in turn, can lead to lower levels of cortisol, the stress hormone, and increased secretion of oxytocin, occasionally called the 'love hormone,' which fosters trust and social bonding.

From a personal growth standpoint, compassionate love holds practical value—it's not merely an adornment of the human spirit. It has been postulated that the ability to care deeply for others without immediate personal gain separates us from other species. Acts of compassion strengthen communal ties, creating networks of reciprocity that can be crucial in times of need.

In the psychological realm, compassion is an emotional response that entails noticing others' suffering and a desire to help. Researchers argue that compassionate love involves recognizing oneself in another and understanding that vulnerability is a shared human condition. This feeling translates into actions that strive to alleviate the pain of others, which is a cornerstone of functioning societies.

Empirical evidence supporting the health benefits of compassionate love also exists in abundance. Researchers have found associations between compassionate love and reduced blood pressure, lowered risk of heart disease, and even increased longevity. Caring for others can, quite literally, mend and sustain our hearts.

The connective tissue of compassionate love lies in empathy, the psychological mechanism that allows one to feel another's emotional state. Empathy has been a subject of fascination in psychological studies, revealing its critical role in compassionate love. It facilitates understanding and care, bridging individual gaps and creating a platform for shared experiences.

Moreover, theories from developmental psychology suggest that compassionate love is not a static trait but a capacity that can be nurtured from infancy. Secure attachments during childhood lay the groundwork for developing empathy and exhibiting compassionate love. As such, the seeds for a loving world are sown in the formative years of our lives.

Social scientists investigating communal living and cooperative societies find that compassionate love drives harmony and conflict resolution. In these studies, merciful love translates into tangible outcomes such as collaborative problem-solving and reduced social tensions. Hence, the impact of compassionate love extends beyond personal well-being; it is pivotal to the cohesion and resilience of communities.

Additionally, findings in the burgeoning field of positive psychology emphasize the enriching nature of compassionate love. Researchers in this field argue that human love empowers individuals, allowing them to transcend their limitations and achieve greater personal fulfillment and life satisfaction. We can enhance overall well-being by cultivating positive traits, including compassionate love.

While discussing the scientific aspects of compassionate love, it is crucial to understand that while science offers quantitative analysis, the qualitative depth of this phenomenon travels beyond mere data. Studies may quantify trends and neurochemical changes, yet the lived experience of compassionate love bleeds into the tapestry of life, painting it with hues of care, warmth, and selflessness that elude numerical capture.

This interplay between the personal and the biological, the subjective and the objective, unveils the multidimensional landscape of love. When we contemplate compassionate love through the prism of science, it becomes evident that our capacity to love compassionately is inextricably linked to our very biology and psyche. Yet, its expression is as individual as a fingerprint, as unique as every human's narrative.

The potential for compassionate love is vast and varied. As a trait, it is as old as humanity itself, and its roots burrowed deep in social behaviors that have allowed our species to thrive. Modern science is revealing that by embracing these behaviors—by nurturing compassionate love—we're not just enriching individual lives. We're contributing to the health and vitality of all humanity.

In sum, the scientific perspectives on compassionate love offer illuminative insights, revealing it to be a potent force for good, a necessity rather than a luxury. As we understand love in its many forms, this knowledge can be a beacon, guiding us toward the kind of love that asks for nothing in return. This love truly serves the love that underpins the most incredible accomplishment of humankind.

In embracing science's revelations about compassionate love, we grasp a vital truth: love encompasses much more than feelings. It is an active process, a choice manifesting in service and kindness. Recognizing this is a stepping stone to unwrapping the misconceptions that shroud our understanding of love, guiding us toward a pathway of genuine connection and sustained altruism.

Putting Compassion into Practice

Having traversed through the scientific landscapes of compassionate love, we find ourselves at the precipice of transformation, where knowledge, rich with potential, clamors for action. Compassion's voice, though gentle, is insistent, urging us not to sit amid the abstract but to rise and embody its very essence in the tangible world around us. It's here, in the denseness of daily life, that compassion finds its fullest expression, and love becomes not just an emotion felt but a service rendered.

To commence this vital transition from understanding to living, we must first recognize that compassion is not merely a passive sentiment. It requires awakening to the plight of others with a willingness to act. It's neither a sporadic kindness nor a convenient gesture. To authentically put compassion into practice, we must weave it into everyday interactions.

Envision the multitude of moments ripe with opportunity—a word of encouragement to someone teetering on the edge of despair, perhaps, or a meal shared with one who knows the gnawing of hunger. These are the threads of compassion that, when knitted together, form a tapestry of goodwill encircling humanity.

The journey commences in the realm of attentiveness. Keen observation becomes our ally, for how can we address the needs of others if we're blind to their presence? One must cultivate the habit of seeing beyond oneself—to notice the quiet struggles and silent pleas for kindness that otherwise go unheeded. In this, we become guardians of empathy, ready to take up the baton of caring deeds.

Amid the clamor of life, one might find the concept of active listening obscured. Yet, hearing the said and unsaid is critically essential in practicing compassion. Beyond the utility of language, active listening echoes the heart's language, discerning the emotions that words sometimes fail to capture. It's a sanctuary of understanding where individuals feel acknowledged and valued.

Delving into the essence of altruism, we realize that genuine compassion involves sacrifice. It is giving when inconvenient, extending a hand even when it means we may momentarily falter. The expectation of reciprocity does not taint the purity of our intention. Instead, it thrives in the joy of lightening another's burden, regardless of what it may cost us.

As our empathy deepens, so too does our capacity for kindness. Small acts become infused with extraordinary significance. Whether lending an ear to a friend or volunteering time for a community project, each gesture of compassion weaves into the communal spirit, immersing us in the shared human experience.

Compassion finds sustenance to grow when we dress in the robes of patience. It understands that change is incremental and that the seeds of kindness we plant today may only blossom in the fullness of time. Patience is the quiet nurturer of hope, standing firm through storm and drought.

One might mistake compassion as solely the domain of grand, heroic actions. Yet, genuine compassion is often most radiant in the quietness of modest service. The consistency of kind acts—holding the door, offering a smile, providing a gentle word—builds the tower of a compassionate life.

However, one cannot pour from an empty cup. Thus, self-care becomes intrinsic to the practice of compassion. Appreciating our humanity, with its spectrum of needs and limits, positions us to give more fully to others. Self-care is not an indulgence—it's the vessel's maintenance through which compassion flows.

To anchor compassionate love in the real, we might create reflection moments to ponder the impact of our actions and rebalance our intentions. Reflective practice keeps our motivations clear and our desire to serve untainted by ego or insincerity. The compass guides our compassionate journey, ensuring we stay on course amidst the labyrinth of life's distractions.

Moreover, to sustain compassion, we must celebrate it within communities. Sharing stories of compassion and recognizing acts of kindness within our circles amplifies their influence. It creates ripples that extend far beyond the initial act, encouraging a culture where compassion is admired, aspired to, and replicated.

Lastly, the practice of gratitude illuminates the path of compassion. When we're thankful for the love and kindness we've received, it fuels our desire to give back. It's a cyclical dance of give-and-take perpetuating an ecosystem of empathy, crafting a world where love is less of a whispered wish and more of an entrenched ethos.

And so, the practice of compassion, resembling a mosaic of small but priceless pieces, becomes an artful endeavor. We're each an artist in our own right, with the power to add beauty to the canvas of existence. Through our everyday gestures, sustained by mindfulness, sacrifice, and patience, compassion becomes not just a concept but a resounding heartbeat in the symphony of life.

Chapter 10:
Is Love a Feeling or Serving?

In the preceding chapters, we've journeyed through the multifaceted landscape of love, dissecting its cultural evolution and addressing common misconceptions. As we delve deeper into the essence of this enigmatic force in Chapter 10, we grapple with a poignant inquiry: Is love a mere cascade of feelings, or is it the selfless act of serving? With their transient and ephemeral nature, feelings paint love as a fleeting high, a momentary bliss that vanishes as quickly as it surfaces. However, viewing love through the lens of service unveils a profound truth: love transcends the realm of transient emotions, manifesting as a steadfast commitment to nurture, care, and hold space for another's growth. This undying devotion, this tireless philanthropy of the soul, frames love as an unwavering choice, a conscious daily decision to walk in empathy and sacrifice. It prompts us to question, when the initial ember of passion dims, what remains? Is it not the acts of service, the silent yet substantial threads that weave individuals together, forming a tapestry more resilient than mere emotion? As we explore the dance between emotion and choice, between feelings and service, we uncover love's most authentic form—a blend where the heart's spontaneous stirrings are matched equally by the stoic resolve to serve.

Emotions and Choices in Love As our exploration of love delves ever more profoundly, we recognize that it is not merely a static state but a dynamic interplay between what we feel and how we choose to act. The heart, enigmatic and fervent, commands a powerful influence, but it is the conscious choices that give love its proper form and expression. The path of love, winding and diverse, is tinted with a spectrum of emotions that stir within us, each painting a portrait of the motivations that drive us forward or the fears that hold us back.

The emotions we term 'love' are complex and often uncontrollable surges that envelop us, perceived as the heart's true calling. They form the initial threads that tug us toward one another; they are the sparks that ignite passion, kindle romance, and foster the desire for intimacy. However, they are also erratic, subject to the ebbs and flows of our psychological state and the external pressures exerted by our environment.

Even within this storm of feelings, choices surface. They are the anchor points that allow love to mature beyond mere feeling. It's a misconception to perceive love solely as an uncontrollable force that sweeps us away. Instead, the daily decisions and the commitment to cherish, communicate, and compromise elevate emotion to enduring love.

Consider the deliberate choice to embrace vulnerability; it is not a passive acquiescence to chance but an active engagement with uncertainty. In revealing our true selves, we commit acts of bravery, trusting not only in the strength of our emotions but also in our choice to be genuine in the presence of our beloved.

Respect plays its part, also from feelings of admiration and a conscious determination to honor the other's humanity, dreams, and flaws. It is a decision made repeatedly in moments of conflict and in times of peace. Love that lacks the choice of respect teeters on the precipice of becoming shallow and fleeting.

Forgiveness is another choice essential to the constellation of love. Emotions can lead our hearts to become barricaded behind grudges, yet forgiving paves a pathway to reconciliation and understanding. As we opt for forgiveness over resentment, love evolves from a naïve sentiment to a resilient bond that can weather storms.

Gratitude, often overlooked, is a choice that nourishes the soul of love. Recognizing and appreciating the value of the other, their actions, and their presence cannot be left solely to the whims of feeling grateful when happenstance dictates. Instead, actively seeking and acknowledging these joys consolidates the foundation of a loving relationship.

This journey through love insists on honesty – a blend of emotional intuition and deliberate truthfulness. Without the chosen sincerity to accurately convey our inner worlds, emotions can mislead, creating rifts where there should be bridges. Honesty fortifies trust and deepens the intimacy that emotions have kindled.

Yet, conflicts inevitably arise within the turbulence of emotions and the steadfastness of choice. Here, love is tested rigorously, not in the heights of passion or depths of despair, but in the arena where choices clash with raw feelings. In these moments, love's true nature is revealed, as the choice to seek understanding and harmony speaks volumes over the silent brooding of hurt emotions.

And as love matures, so the role of choices becomes increasingly critical. Long-term relationships are neither sustained by chance nor by the unrelenting force of initial passions but are carefully crafted through our daily decisions – to listen, share, support, and grow together. In this light, love becomes an art form where emotions inspire, but choices create the masterpiece.

When assessing love's merit, we must ask: are we truly listening to our emotions or allowing them to rule us unchecked? Emotions may guide us, but it is the steady hand of choice that carries us toward a love that is both deep and real. While emotions are the threads of color that paint our experiences, choice is the brush that shapes the pattern of our shared tapestry of love.

In times of hardship, the decisions to persevere, be patient, and show kindness bind partners together more than the erratic nature of feeling alone. These determined efforts epitomize the serving nature of love—a service to the other, the relationship, and ultimately, the growth of both individuals intertwined within its bond.

Love is not an effortless voyage; it demands a steadfast captain at the helm—our ability to choose. We cannot leave our destinations to the currents of emotion alone but must navigate using heart and mind. The nuanced amalgamation of emotions and choices in love creates a magnificently human journey with all its beauty and imperfections.

This section beckons us to embrace the philosophy that love is more than a passive state of being. It is a series of active choices that, when aligned with our emotions, can forge a connection that is as enduring as it is heartfelt. Therein lies the genuine service of love—the commitment to continuously choose what nourishes, sustains, and elevates the essence of our shared humanity through love.

To pursue love is to engage both the heart's passions and the mind's resolutions. It's to understand that while emotions are the melody of love's song, our choices are the harmonies that give it depth and sustainability. As we navigate the complex dance of emotions and choices in love, we create a symphony that endures beyond the fleeting whispers of transitory feelings—a symphony scored by the countless little yet monumental choices we make for love.

Service as an Expression of Love Once we peel away the layers of misconception surrounding love, we unveil a profound truth - that, at its core, love manifests as service. Far from being a simple surge of affection or the dizzying height of romance, real love encompasses acts of service that reinforce and communicate our commitment.

The fabric of love is woven through daily choices and actions that prioritize another's happiness and well-being. When offered selflessly, voluntary service emerges as a delicate yet powerful articulation of love. It's a concept that transcends cultures and echoes through the ages, whispering that genuine affection is demonstrated through deeds rather than declared through words alone.

Consider love as a verb, an action that, when performed with sincerity, can transform both the giver and the receiver. Service - giving oneself for the betterment of another - is a hallmark of this active form of love. It requires us to stretch beyond our comfort zones, to give without expectation of return, and to find joy in the joy of others.

To serve another person in the name of love is to acknowledge their worth and dignity. It's a silent covenant that says, "You are important, and I am here for you." This service can take countless forms, from the grand gestures to the minutiae of daily life. Making a loved one's favorite meal, tending to a sick friend, or volunteering one's time and resources for a partner's project; each act bolsters the intangible bond of love.

In relationships, mundane tasks often become the very expression of our affection. Laundry is folded, dishes are washed, and errands run - not chores but love made visible. When one pours love into such services, the mundane transmutes into the sacred. The routine care for our shared spaces and lives becomes a dance of mutual respect and admiration.

Service in love is also about emotional availability and the offering of support during trying times. Being present during moments of vulnerability or hardship is an emblem of a strong affection that isn't swayed by the ebbs and flows of circumstance. It steadies us, offering a harbor in the tumultuous seas of life.

Moreover, service in love has an uncanny ability to cut through the noise of daily life, focusing our attention on what truly matters. In a society that often confuses love for possession or status, acts of service remind us that love is something you do, not something you have. As we engage in loving service, we let go of superficial measures of love and embrace a more enduring, meaningful expression.

The ethos of service in love is transformative. As we give of ourselves, we often receive much more in return - not necessarily from those we serve but through the rich, internal reward of personal growth and happiness. Knowing that our actions have lightened another's burden or brightened another's day is a profound joy.

Notably, service as an expression of love isn't about subservience or losing oneself in the needs of others. It's a conscious choice that fosters a balanced relationship where reciprocity isn't an obligation but a natural outcome of genuine care and affection. This equilibrium is the cornerstone of a healthy love that endures.

This isn't to say that service should be performed with the expectation of reciprocity. The purity of service in love lies in its unconditional nature. It's about giving because it embodies your feelings and respect, not because you anticipate a reward or acknowledgment. Where love is the motivation, service transcends transactions and becomes a testament to our capacity for selflessness.

Delving into history, we find luminaries who have encapsulated this philosophy in their lives. Their stories inspire us to view service not as a mere act but as a way of living and loving. It's an aspiration to elevate our most cherished relationships into spaces where the beloved's welfare becomes as imperative as one's own.

In summary, service is the unseen thread that strengthens the bond of love between individuals. It's a testament to the depth and maturity of our affection. And while service is to be celebrated in all its forms, it's not the grandeur but the intent that imbues it with the essence of love. As we adopt this perspective, we understand that the most potent declarations of love are often not draped in extravagance but nestled in the tranquility of everyday service.

Embracing this embodiment of love requires a shift in perspective. One must recognize that every moment offers an opportunity to express love through service. This realization invites us to look beyond ourselves, ensuring our relationships are maintained and nourished by a love that is as generous as it is profound.

Indeed, service as an expression of love is a choice and lifestyle. In the act of giving - of time, attention, and care - we find the purest form of connection with another. Through service, love is no longer a noun but a verb, actively shaping the world around us and the bonds we treasure.

Chapter 11:
Love's Lifecycle: From Infatuation to Maturity

In the long and winding journey from the first flush of infatuation to the gentle, deep-rooted growth of mature love lies a path less illuminated by the spotlight, yet more enduring than the brief glow of passion, as a tender bud contends with the elements to blossom, so does love transition through seasons - from the spring of ardor to the winter of contentment - its survival dependent on the nurturing of mutual respect, the cultivation of shared experiences, and the resilience of unwavering commitment. Within the tapestry of interwoven lives, love is invariably tested by time and tribulation, tasked to transcend the dizzying heights of initial infatuation and to find a foothold in the rich, fertile ground of trust and intimate familiarity. It's a transition that dispels naive fantasies, urging one's heart to beat in accordance with another through the symphony of life's vicissitudes, each crescendo and decrescendo a testimony to love's transcendent power. In this chapter, we explore this transformative odyssey, recognizing that love, in its most accurate form, is a dynamic, lived experience, an enduring labor of growth that requires both partners to serve one another, cultivating a bond that can weather the inevitable storms it will face.

The Stages of Love in Relationships unfold like a journey through the fabric of our being, touching every chord of the soul, challenging the heart's resilience, and shaping our most profound perceptions. It's an odyssey that often starts with a spark, an instant magnetism that draws two people into a ballet of feelings. This enthusiasm, which society often glorifies, is the infancy of love's lifecycle—the infatuation stage, where the heart races and palms sweat at the mere thought of the beloved.

In this stage, love wears a mask of idealization; every action and word is tinted with the rose color of perfection. The world seems brighter, food tastes better, and music carries more weight. It is the stuff of poetry and prose, the whirlwind romances that fairytales are made of. But one must pause and consider—is this the entirety of love's domain?

As the chapters of time add pages to the story of a relationship, love begins to peel back its layers, revealing a more sobering reality. Partners start to notice quirks and flaws in each other, recognizing the undeniable humanity beneath the polished veneer. This stage is confronting and beckons for a deeper contemplation of the notion of love. Is it just the emotional highs, or is it something more?

Following the threshold of awakening comes the test of adjustment and accommodation. Two individuals learn to dance synchronously, not only to the rhythm of joy but also through the quieter moments and the disarray of misunderstandings. Here, love calls for patience and an understanding that echoes beyond mere acceptance; it is about the metamorphosis of feeling into action—where serving intertwines with the raw emotions of love.

The very fibers of what we perceive as love are reshaped as couples embark upon the journey of togetherness, where love begins to don the roles of respect, sacrifice, and support. Bonds are forged in the fires of daily life, stoking a warmth that is less about fleeting sparks and more about a consistent glow—the transition from romance to companionship.

In the heart of the relationship, the stage of deep connection emerges. It's a quieter, more profound realization of love that doesn't clamor for attention with high passion but whispers in the mundane acts of living together. It's found in the rhythm of routines, the comfort of silent companionship, and the unspoken understanding that year after year, two people have a choice and choose each other.

It's here we pause to reflect—is love merely emotion? Or is it the choice to extend oneself, day after day, for the well-being of the other? The ebb and flow of feelings are intrinsic to our existence, but the constancy of choice and action anchors love in reality. Serving becomes the language through which love articulates itself beyond words or sentiments.

The subsequent stages of love require a coalition of courage, commitment, and the deliberate act of nurturing the burgeoning sprout that has grown from infatuation to a more seasoned adoration. With this commitment comes the need for forgiveness, the willingness to work through conflicts, and the determination to see through the lens of long-term devotion over temporary satisfaction.

Love's maturity is the accumulation of time spent together and an active, daily pursuit of harmony. It's a labor, not a feeling that wanes with the moon's phases, but a steadfast sentinel, guarding the relationship against the storm of life's trials and tribulations. It is the understanding that love is less about possessing and more about giving freely.

As relationships continue to weave their narrative through the years, love settles into a form seldom celebrated in sonnets or on the silver screen. It is the unglamorous sustenance of each other's dreams, sharing in losses and triumphs, and the interspersion of lives so intricate that the individual melodies form a single symphony of togetherness. This is the unison stage, where lives are not just shared but melded into a single entity with a shared history, present, and future.

Perhaps the most profound stage is what could be termed the legacy of love. It is the mark a relationship leaves on those within its circle, a testament to the power of love manifest in actions over words. This legacy is the intangible impression that influences the next generation, teaching by example what it means to love, serve, and remain steadfast through life's vicissitudes.

Understanding the stages of love in relationships reveals that love, in its truest sense, must evolve from the emotional to the actionable. Feelings may ignite the journey, but the conscious decision to serve, to put someone else's needs alongside or even above one's own, fuels the enduring flame of love.

Thus, love becomes not just a feeling to be passively experienced but a series of deliberate choices, actions, and sacrifices. Each stage of love asks anew: "What does love require of me now?" And at every turning point, the answer is found in serving—not as a chore or burden but as the most authentic expression of love itself.

As we travel through the stages of love, we learn that the journey is not meant to be a solo voyage but a shared expedition, where serving the other becomes the beacon that guides us through uncharted waters. Love is ultimately about our choices to connect, persevere, and dedicate our actions to the welfare of the one we claim to hold dear.

In navigating these stages, love is not static; it is an evolving testament to an individual's character and commitment. Both the quiet moments and the tempestuous trials sculpt love's proper form. Serving as an expression of love becomes a testament to the depth of the connection, the authenticity of the sentiment, and the resilience of a bond that can weather all seasons of life.

From Passion to Deep Connection As we voyage through life's complex tapestry, intertwining threads of emotion and experience, one of the most profound transitions we navigate is the evolution of love in our intimate relationships. In its infancy, love often ignites as a bright, consuming flame known as passion. This fiery beginning is sometimes mistaken as the pinnacle of love's journey, yet it is a prelude to something deeper, a portal to a profound connection.

Passion can be as tumultuous as a stormy sea—exhilarating, intense, yet potentially fleeting. It's an initial magnetic pull between souls, a unity sculpted by desire and longing. But the depth of love unfolds only when this fervor matures into a more comprehensive bond, woven by strands of shared experiences, challenges surmounted together, and the quiet nourishment of mutual support.

A deep connection diverges from passion as it doesn't rely on the constant presence of intensity. It thrives on a stable foundation where trust is the cornerstone. In this forge, love becomes an enduring presence, as resilient as the mountains weathering the tests of time and the elements.

To flourish from passion to deep connection takes conscious effort and heartful commitment. It can't be left to the whims of chance or the idle passing of seasons. It would be best if you nurtured it with care, fed it with kindness, and protected it with unwavering devotion.

It is a myth that love does not require work. Any gardener will tell you that the most beautiful flower beds need the most attentive cultivation. Similarly, love's transition from a passionate flame to a steady warmth demands diligence and patience, watering the roots with acts of service and the company of compassionate conversations that stretch into the night.

As you journey from the spark of new love into the depths of connection, you discover that love is less about ceaseless emotion and more about concerted action. Serving your partner becomes a testament to your commitment, a living expression of a dynamic love that moves well beyond mere feeling.

Genuine connection thrives when partners become attentive to the whispers of one another's needs, often unspoken yet deeply felt. Tender gestures, a look that communicates volumes, and the silent giving of support without thought of return are the currencies of a deeply connected love.

In this haven, vulnerability transforms into strength. Revealing your true self is not an act of weakness but rather the ultimate demonstration of trust. The exchange of dreams, fears, and unguarded moments is the fertile soil in which intimacy flourishes.

When the initial blaze of passion settles into glowing embers, many fear that love has waned. Yet, if cared for, those embers provide a sustained heat that warms you from within. They hold the potential to ignite new flames, ones that burn steadily and give light to paths previously untraveled.

How does one discern if passion has matured into this deeper connection? It's found in the serenity of partnership, where silence speaks louder than words and presence more poignant than grand gestures. It is felt when adversity is faced not as a splitter of union but as an opportunity for growth, drawing you closer in solidarity.

This transition can be as subtle as the changing seasons. You may not notice the precise moment when the fiery hues of autumn give way to winter's serene whiteness, but at some point, you'll find yourself basking in the profound peace that comes with enduring love.

In this deep connection, whether love is a feeling or serving becomes redundant. It is both—a feeling that inspires you to serve and a service that continually stirs the feelings of love. Through each act, through every tender word, the connection deepens, and the true essence of love is revealed.

Amid this confluence, love becomes its most authentic self—not just an emotion to be chased but a choice to be made daily. Choosing to love through the mundane, to find the extraordinary in the ordinary, is the hallmark of a bond that has transitioned from the brief to the eternal.

In this structure, communication is not merely about speaking but confirming your partner's value, ensuring they are seen and heard. It is about reaffirming your commitment to understanding their world as keenly as your own, even as it reshapes and evolves.

Thus, let us not idealize passion to the extent that we neglect the beauty of deep connection. For the latter is a sanctuary for our most human need—to be known, accepted, and loved without the fear that love might someday recede with the falling tides of emotion. In the deep connection, love is not just a spontaneous combustion of feeling; it becomes the deliberate choice to keep the glow alive, an intimate dance between two souls in a harmonious and enduring waltz.

Chapter 12:
Communication as the Backbone of Love

In the quest to understand love's proper form, we arrive at a profound truth: communication is not merely the exchange of words; it's the bridge that connects the isles of solitude within us. Just as a bridge withstands the vigors of weather and time, communication as the backbone of love demands resilience and undeterred effort. Where emotions ebb and flow like the tide, and service manifests as the tangible structure of devotion, it is in communication that love finds its voice and its echo. Converse is to share not just thoughts but portions of the heart, each word a carrier of hope, a confessor of fears, a celebration of shared joys. The art of listening, its counterpart, is where love's true power lies dormant, waiting to be awakened by the gentlest whisper of genuine understanding. In this chapter, we shall explore the fabric of communication woven with threads of patience, attentiveness, and the unspoken—each as vital as the next. To hold love is to have a conversation that never ceases, where silences are meaningful, and through which we navigate the delicate dance of giving and receiving—one where each step is taken not in solitude but in the respectful company of another's soul.

Understanding Through Words - our journey thus far has indicated that love is as complex as it is simple, as confounding as it is clear. Language, the vessel through which we navigate the vast seas of human connection, bears the undeniable power to draw us closer or set us adrift. Within communication, words act as the compass by which we charter the course of love's intricate dance.

Consider the tale of two souls, aligning and misaligning in the rhythmic cycle of understanding and misunderstanding. Here, we find that love isn't merely an array of feelings to be felt but a myriad of actions to be performed. Among these actions is communication—an offering and receiving of ourselves through language conduit. When we articulate our inner worlds, we present a gift wrapped in vulnerability, inviting others to know us beyond the surface.

It is pertinent to acknowledge that while emotions set the stage, choice guides the actors. We convey respect, admiration, and care in addressing those we love. Conversely, we might succumb to the temptation of harsh words, which, like a cold wind, can quickly extinguish the warm flames of affection. Words, therefore, are the vessels of our intentions, the ambassadors of our wills, bearing the weight of either construction or destruction in our relationships.

In the realm of love, serving becomes an eloquent language spoken not just in grand gestures but whispered in the quiet subtleties of everyday life. To navigate our shared human experience, we employ words to express romantic love and the broader spectrum of connection that defines our social existence. From the gentle encouragement offered to a friend to the tender reassurances given to a child, our words serve as a testament to the depth and sincerity of our concern for others.

A common misconception is that love's most accurate form is found only in the fiery passion of its early stages—the fancy dinners, the poetic praises sung, and the endless declarations of undying affection. But as we peel back the layers of sensationalism painted by modern media, we discover a quieter, more resilient love. One where service becomes an integral part, embodied in the everyday words that build a life together: the "thank you's," the "how was your day's," and the "I'm here for you are."

Language, in its essence, is a bridge. The architecture allows us to traverse the distances between our individual islands of self. When love becomes a verb, its syntax is often constructed with the building blocks of service—the doing, the acting, and the living out of promises made. And how do we convey such action? Through words that align with deeds, through language that echoes our commitment to stand by others in the tapestry of life.

In this symphony of souls intertwining, listening plays its counterpart in the communion of utterances. Recall the echoes of love's calls and responses—the way a phrase tenderly spoken can resonate within the caverns of the heart. Such resonance proves that love's discourse is reciprocal, that we must be as adept in receiving words with openness as we are in offering them with generosity.

Service in love extends beyond the mortal realm into the ethereal domain of language. It's the temperance shown when words are withheld in moments of anger, choosing instead to breathe through the tumult until calm can restore dialogue's potential. Or the conscious choice of affirming language that uplifts rather than diminishes, validating rather than negating the essence of those we love.

To truly understand love is to embrace the full spectrum of its expression. Just as a caring touch can soothe a troubled mind, thoughtful words can mend a weary soul. Within the sanctuary of shared silence and spoken reflections, we affirm our presence in each other's lives. Our words thus can become the very embodiment of service, tending to the garden of affection with the water of wisdom and the light of truth.

Misunderstandings will arise like inevitable storms within the labyrinth of love, casting dark shadows of doubt. It's here, within the storm's eye, that words' power is tested. Do we lash out or use our language to navigate back to a place of mutual understanding? Our words can be the lighthouse guiding us home or the rocks upon which the ship of love shatters.

Let us then be artisans with our words, crafting sentences like delicate pieces of art, which bear the rawness of our feelings yet the precision of our intent. In every "I'm sorry," "I forgive you," and "I am with you," let there be an undercurrent of service, a current that steadfastly flows toward the sea of a more profound and more accurate love.

It has been said that action speaks louder than words, yet sometimes words are the action in the paradox of love. When we convey our commitment, not just in lofty proclamations but in the daily dialogue of life, we exercise a form of service. Our words are not empty vessels but are filled with the substance of our willingness to make love real and tangible.

The threads of affection are woven in the loom of our daily interactions, spun together with every consonant and vowel pronounced in kindness. In this light, service in love does not merely pertain to the physical manifestation of our devotion but to the verbal affirmation of our presence in the lives of those we cherish. Just as love grows within the soil of action, it blossoms under the sunlight of supportive and nourishing words.

In this understanding, this relentless pursuit to define love through our language, we both find and lose ourselves. We discover the power within words to heal, harm, build up, or break down. In this discovery, we are responsible for using our words as a force for good and service to those we value above ourselves.

As we move forward, let us carry with us the understanding that love, in its most profound sense, is the intertwining of feelings and service. It manifests itself graciously in our words, the essence of our intent, and the voice of our actions. Ultimately, the measure of our love will be the legacy of our language—how we use our words to lift, mend, bond, and serve.

Listening: An Act of Love In exploring the labyrinthine nuances of love, we make our way to the sanctuary of listening, one of the most potent yet understated acts that love demands of us. Too often, love is equated with grand gestures or poetic proclamations, but deep within the essence of love's true nature lies the simple act of listening—a silent form of giving that requires the presence of one's entire being.

Listening, in its purest form, is selfless. It's the decision to suspend one's narrative to make room for another's. When performed with genuine attention, this act transforms an ordinary exchange into a sanctum of connection, where the currency is not words but the space between them—the space where understanding and compassion flourish.

To listen is to serve. It is an offering one makes to another. When you hear, you provide a platform for cleansing, for a catharsis of pent-up emotions that may have been aching for release. You become the confessor to someone's silent prayers and unspoken fears. This service is one of love's most tangible expressions. It isn't clad in the guise of romance. It doesn't always play to an audience. Its rewards are not always immediate, yet it is imperative to the symphony of a meaningful relationship.

Listening goes beyond mere quietness in the presence of another's voice. It involves actively engaging the mind, parsing language for meaning and the emotion that imbues it. It requires the listener to read between the lines, to comprehend not just the words but also the tone, the hesitations, and the melody that rides the wave of speech. It demands a total immersion into the moment at hand, undistracted and undivided attention.

In slowing down to truly hear, we engage with our partners' stories and feelings, therefore standing in solidarity with their experiences. This empathetic stance doesn't just hear the story; it feels it. It dances to the rhythm of the teller's heart and understands the silent pauses that punctuate the spoken truths.

Yet, why does listening elude so many when it seemingly asks for so little? It is perhaps because, in the quiet act of listening, one confronts one's inner noise—the tangled thoughts, the judgments waiting to leap forth, the desire to fix rather than hold space. To listen reverently to another, one must first quiet the cacophony within oneself to become a vessel of attention and care.

Love's strength is tested not just in the sharing of joy but in the sharing of sorrow. Words often fail in sorrow's chilly grasp, but a listening heart speaks volumes. It consoles without saying a word, supports without being seen, and validates the harrowing stretch of emotions that grip those we hold dear.

Some believe the ultimate act of love is to sacrifice, but what more tremendous sacrifice is there than yielding one's ego, the relinquishment of the need to be heard in favor of hearing? In the silence of our listening, we lay down a piece of ourselves to uplift another. This sacrifice doesn't demand an altar; it lives in the everyday moments where we choose to be fully present.

Communication forms the keystone in relationships—the element without which the arch crumbles. Suppose words are the stones building this bridge. In that case, listening is the mortar that holds them together, allowing for the safe traverse of our deepest sentiments across the divide of individual experience.

When we listen with the intent to understand rather than to respond, we build an unspoken trust. We tell the other, "Your feelings are valid. Your perspective matters. You matter." This validation is the bedrock upon which a sound relationship is built—one where partners feel seen, heard, and valued.

The art of listening is indeed just that—an art. It is cultivated over time, tended to with patience, and nurtured with intention. It requires practice and humility, for it is not always easy to relinquish center stage, especially if one's instinct is to solve problems or provide solutions. Sometimes, the most profound support lies not in the answers we offer but in the silence, we keep that allows others to find their answers.

Ultimately, listening is an act of surrender. It compels us to set aside our version of the world and enter someone else's. It challenges our preconceptions and opens the door to a diverse landscape of thoughts and emotions that, when truly embraced, enrich us beyond measure.

The fabric of love is woven with countless threads, but none quite as resilient or subtle as the listening strand. To listen is to love actively and assiduously. The invisible embrace can bring solace in tumult, joy in sorrow, and peace in conflict. It is the act of love that asks for nothing yet offers everything.

As we venture forth in our relationships, may we carry with us the understanding that to listen is to allow love to breathe and to thrive. It is the stillness amidst the chaos, the peace amidst the storm. In offering our listening ears, we become the custodians of our loved ones' stories, and in doing so, we take part in the sacred dance of connection, community, and, ultimately, love.

In the grand tapestry of human intimacy, many threads will fray, and many patterns will fade. Still, the incandescent listening thread will always illuminate the path to understanding, empathy, and the unspoken depths of love in the human heart.

Chapter 13:
Overcoming Challenges with Love

In the heart of every enduring relationship, trials emerge as both test and testimony, revealing the essence and strength of the connection. To love genuinely is to recognize that affection extends far beyond emotive fervor; it is a holy form of service, a dedicated pragmatism in the face of life's tumults. As we traverse the dynamic landscape of shared existence, we find conflict and resolution not merely as antagonists but as the co-authors of our narrative, each challenge a brushstroke in the masterpiece of our bond. Within this chapter lies the unwavering conviction that through the crucible of adversity, love does not diminish; rather, it crystallizes, refracting the daily toils into a spectrum of shared growth. The journey through misunderstanding and hurt navigated with patience and a mutual commitment to understanding, becomes a path to a more profound union. It's within the forge of challenges that love is tempered, and from the malleable iron of our togetherness, a resilient bond is wrought, one capable of withstanding the fluctuations of life. This unwavering commitment to face trials hand in hand serves the present and sets the cornerstone for future harmony, crafting a legacy of love that endures. Love's most significant victory is not found in the absence of hardship. Still, the transformation ushers through persistence, empathy, and a shared vision that gleams even in moments of darkness.

Conflict and Resolution in Love

The notion of conflict in love is often seen as the opposition of harmony, and yet it is innate to any dynamic and living relationship. This paradox is how the strength of a bond is tested and the depth of love is measured. Resolution becomes not merely a return to homeostasis but an evolution of the connection between two souls.

When we dare to venture into the realm of love, we're met with an inevitable truth: the heart's journey is paved with moments of discord. While seemingly obstructive, these conflicts serve a purpose far more significant than discomfort—they are the impetus for growth and understanding. Like the strain that forges steel, love's challenges can strengthen the bonds between us if navigated with care.

In examining love's skirmishes, it is vital to recognize that conflict is often born from a disparity in perspectives, desires, or needs. It is the interplay of individual intricacies that, when aligned harmoniously, create a symphony but, when in dissonance, result in strife. Love, in its essence, calls on us to embrace this diversity, honoring the other's truths as we seek common ground.

To untangle the knots of confrontation, communication is a sentinel guarding the gateway to resolution. It requires an unwavering commitment to express oneself openly and listen receptively. Love speaks in tender whispers and unspoken gestures, asking us to perceive the silent cries as much as the spoken words.

Resolution is not simply a matter of compromise or concession; it is a more profound recognition and integration of each other's essence into a more expansive understanding of love. It challenges us to stand in the cradle of vulnerability, shining a light on our shadows, and ultimately, it asks for forgiveness—both of the self and the beloved.

Through the lens of love's complexities, we also unravel the thread of expectations. Our vision of perfect harmony often clashes with the reality of human imperfection. By redefining our outlook to see the beauty in the imperfect, we discover the potency of love's authentic expression, which is neither faultless nor constant but resilient and adaptive.

As we journey together, the remnants of conflicts witness our passage toward unity. They are the scars that tell tales of survivals and conquests, not of battles between foes, but of lovers striving for a greater communion. Resolutions are the shared victories in love's odyssey, celebrations of having weathered the storm and emerging not apart but closer, with a firmer grasp on each other's hearts.

Still, we must acknowledge that conflict, however frequently it might be resolved, can exact a toll on the spirit. The fabric of our connections can grow thin and weary if we do not mend it with care. Service to one another, an expression of love in its purest form, acts as the thread that repairs and embellishes the tapestry of our shared experiences.

When we serve from a place of love, our actions become the balm to heal wounds and the foundation on which trust is solidified. It is in the daily ritual of serving—be it through acts of kindness, words of encouragement, or the simple gift of presence—that love transcends the ephemeral and becomes tangible.

Love's paradoxical nature reveals that the act of serving may, at times, mean stepping back to allow space for individual growth. In the throes of conflict, love is best expressed by honoring the journey of the other. As much as we yearn to meld our paths, love recognizes the sacredness of the separate vacations contributing to our shared story.

As we learn to navigate conflict with grace and seek resolution with an open heart, we embrace the true serving nature of love—a love that does not dominate or demand but cherishes and uplifts. This is where love transitions from feeling to action, where the temporary ecstasy of emotion is grounded in the concrete manifestations of care and support.

Embracing the truth that conflict is an inherent aspect of love's dynamic allows us to cast off the shackles of unrealistic expectations. We can then honor each stormy passage as an opportunity to deepen our understanding, fortify our connections, and, ultimately, serve love's noble purpose.

As we edge ever closer to love's core through the resolution of myriad conflicts, we begin to perceive love not as a destination but as a sacred journey. It is a journey punctuated by peaks and valleys, each etching a greater capacity for compassion, resilience, and profound companionship into our beings.

This journey, as winding and arduous as it may be, is replete with revelations about the human spirit and the limitless power of love when wielded with intention and grace. In each moment of discord and each act of resolution, love is refined and redefined—reshaped into forms that transcend our initial understanding of it.

Conclusion, then, is not found in escaping conflict nor in seeking a utopian absence of friction. Instead, the proper resolution of love lies in embracing each encounter with open arms, knowing that within the heart of every conflict lies the opportunity for love to flourish in ways previously unimagined. In this space, love becomes an expansive force that elevates us beyond mere feelings—it becomes the ultimate act of serving something greater than ourselves.

Growing Together Through Adversity There is something profoundly transformative about the struggles life throws into the path of love. Adversity is not simply a series of obstacles to be overcome but rather the crucible within which the mettle of a relationship is tested and shaped. When faced with adversity, love can either fracture under the weight of trials or forge an unyielding bond that stands resilient against life's storms.

Consider the role of adversity not as the antagonist in the narrative of a relationship but as the catalyst for growth. Trials, be it financial, health-related, or born from the nuances of interpersonal complexities, have the uncanny ability to strip away the superficial. In moments of crisis, the depth of devotion is revealed and can be nurtured to become the bedrock upon which a couple may build their united front against the world's slings and arrows.

Love's true nature is revealed within the fiery forge of conflict and trial; it is not merely an emotion to be felt but a commitment to be lived. As partners navigate the stormy seas, each wave of difficulty demands choices manifesting their bond's essence. Serving one another in need is the embodiment of love, a tangible action that speaks louder than whispered affections in the calm.

The seeds of understanding are sown in the dark soil of distress. Partners learn about the strengths they didn't know they possessed and the vulnerabilities they didn't think they had. This duality of power and fragility intertwines, creating a more profound sense of empathy that is only achievable through shared experiences of hardship.

A deepened empathy heralds the emergence of altruism within the context of love. As partners witness each other's struggles, an instinct to alleviate pain and enhance the well-being of the other comes to the fore. It's an instinct that underpins compassionate love—the desire not only to receive love but to give it unreservedly, especially when it's most needed.

In the heat of adversity, communication takes on new dimensions. Words may sometimes fail, but earnestly striving to understand and be understood cements the foundation of a resilient relationship. The serenity of listening, truly listening, becomes an unspoken dialogue where support is provided not by mere speech but by presence.

Through adversity, illusions of love are shattered, revealing the stark reality of truly loving someone. Love's honed into something unequivocally real, not in grand gestures or flawless storybook romances but in the mundane and the mire of life's struggles. It's easy to profess love in the golden sun; it's another to stand steadfast in the howling gale.

Compromise is the dance two lovers learn as they navigate through their trials. They discover that stubbornness only deepens divisions, whereas flexibility and a willingness to adapt become the harmonious movements that lead to progression. These dances are workshops of patience and sacrifice, where each beat of hardship choreographs the steps toward unity.

Forgiveness must be woven into a relationship that aims to grow through adversity. To err is human, but to forgive, within the throes of turmoil, is a sublime act that elevates love above the corrosive effects of resentment. It's a sacred release, permitting partners to move forward without the burdens of past grievances shadowing their steps.

Trust is fortified in the furnace of adversity as assurances and promises are met with action. When one partner falls, the other becomes the pillar of support, and through such acts, the foundation of trust becomes as unshakable as the earth beneath their feet. Trust becomes a living entity, grown and fed by each overcoming, each solidarity in the face of adversity.

In the trials landscape, variety is spawned; repeated challenges are never quite the same. Each one calls for a bespoke, tailored strategy that equips partners with an evolving skill set. Just as nature thrives on diversity, so does love grow more vibrant and resilient through the assortment of difficulties faced and conquered.

As they emerge from each adversity, rejuvenated and bonded closely by their shared victories and defeats, partners co-author a narrative of endurance. Their story may not be one that would stir audiences with swooning passion, but rather, it will stand as a testament to perseverance, a beacon for those on similar journeys.

Service to one another becomes a unifying purpose when adversity strikes. It shifts the focus from individual suffering to shared battles. In the solemn pledge to support each other, partners embody the ultimate act of service—placing the relationship's needs above their own, translating love into action.

And so, with each storm weathered together, the true meaning of love unveils itself. It's not just the warmth of affection or the sweetness of romance—it is the unspoken promise, the action taken, the understanding deepened, and the bond fortified. Love is not just a feeling to be savored; it is a service to be rendered—a commitment to hold firm, to carry on side by side, and most crucially, to grow together through every shade of adversity.

The arc of love reveals its full glory not within the confines of serenity but amidst the whirlwind of life's trials. Adversity does not merely test love; it refines it, solidifying a connection that can withstand the vicissitudes of time. It's a journey of consistent, persistent, prolonged, sustained dedicated commitment: a constellation of acts of voluntary service and a unified advancement toward a more profound, indestructible love. This is the nurturing ground where love transcends feeling and becomes an ungovernable force, propelling us together into the boundlessness of a love that serves without limits and endures without end.

Chapter 14:
Creating a Lasting Bond

The journey of love meanders through the meadows of tenderness and the thorny thickets of trials. Yet, its true essence is found not merely in fleeting rapture or stoic endurance but in the conscious construction of an enduring tapestry woven with the threads of commitment and consistency. "Creating a Lasting Bond" is an ode to the grit of love, an exploration into the unspoken covenant that transforms love from a whispering feeling into a monument of serving. This chapter provides pragmatic tools to fortify and nurture love, crafting resilient relationships against the erosion of time and circumstance. It lays bare the profound truth that, beyond the euphoric highs and abysmal lows, the fabric of a sustained love is a meticulously crafted piece, pieced together with daily acts of care, understanding, and the mutual dedication to grow in unison, branches of the same tree reaching for the sky, roots entwined deep within the nurturing earth of shared experiences.

Commitment and Consistency have always been pivotal pillars in the architectural design of enduring love. As we explore these twin concepts, we discover that love is not merely a serendipitous occurrence but the fruit of deliberate actions and ongoing choices. The tapestry of love, woven through commitment and strengthened by Consistency, speaks volumes of its quality and sustainability. To consider love a mere byproduct of feelings is to ignore the sturdy framework upon which lasting relationships are built.

The nature of commitment in love paints the portrait of a decision—a pledge to hold steadfast in the face of life's storms. This unwavering stance is a testament to the value ascribed to the beloved. Commitment in love is often celebrated in glorious ceremonies and vows, yet its genuine essence lies in the quiet, everyday decisions to choose each other anew. These consistently made choices forge a bond that withstands fickle emotions that may flutter and fade with time.

Consistency, the close companion to commitment, is the steady heartbeat of love's existence. The reliability of affection, the predictability of support, and the rhythm of actions match spoken intentions. Much like the sun's rise and set, Consistency in love offers reassurance and establishes a basis of trust, fostering an environment where love can flourish organically.

Imagine love as a garden, where commitment is planting seeds with hope and intention, and Consistency is the diligent tending—the watering and the weeding—required to see those seeds blossom into stunning flora. Without these essential practices, the garden withers, a metaphor for love's potential demise if left untended by these twin guardians.

In service, we find love's true manifestation. Actions, done in commitment and carried out with Consistency, reveal that love is not passive. It is active participation in the well-being of the other. Serving one another, in small ways and grand gestures alike, requires a dedication that surpasses the clamor of fleeting emotions, anchoring love in acts of sacrifice and consideration.

Scrutinize the tapestries of enduring romances spun in the looms of history; they all share threads of staunch commitment and unwavering Consistency. Love that stands the test of time is iridescent with tales of partners who chose to stay together, adapt, and surmount life's challenges through these principles. As we traverse the complexities of human interactions, we are reminded that love's depth is measured not by the eloquence of words professed but by the steadiness of actions displayed.

Consistency also implies a rhythm to the relationship; it helps form shared experiences and traditions that become the bedrock upon which love is continuously rebuilt and reinforced. As these traditions are honored and repeated, they become the unique language of a couple's love, a syntax of affection understood by the two hearts involved.

While society often glorifies the enthusiasm of new love, the quiet fortitude of commitment gets overshadowed. Yet, within this resilience, we uncover the richness of mature love. When passion's flames temper, the glowing ember of connection remains—a warmth sustained by the collective experiences and reaffirmed choices that characterize a committed relationship.

Despite love's idyllic depictions in sonnets and scripts, its true habitat is found in the soil of resolve and the climate of continuity. Love is the labor of patient cultivation and the harvest of mutual respect that matures across seasons. We must recognize that the sentimentality of love is not enough to cross the chasms that life may cast along our path; the bridge of commitment and the sturdy cables of Consistency carry us over.

The notion of serving within love's domain elevates it beyond an emotion to be experienced. It redefines love as an ongoing venture, an expedition wherein lovers become explorers, architects, and artists of their own saga through the acts of giving and supporting one another. This pivot from passive receivership to active contribution shapes the enduring narrative of love.

Events of discord are inevitable in the landscape of any relationship. Here, commitment and Consistency emerge not as suggestions but as imperatives. When love is tested, the resolve to stay the course becomes the compass that recalibrates the journey. Every step taken together through adversity reinforces the bond, solidifying the commitment made during more leisurely times.

It offers a counter-narrative of intentional and steadfast connection in a world that predicates many relationships on the contingency of continued personal happiness or mere chance. The construct of love is not sustained by an invisible hand but by the deliberate choice to remain attached to it against the grain of impermanent desires and in the direction of a shared and intentional future.

Let us then embrace love's call to constancy with the same enthusiasm with which we embrace the fleeting whims of passion. To cast love in the mold of service—committed and consistent—is to shape it into a vessel that can journey across the ocean of time. The masterpiece of love is not found in the grand overture but in the quiet symphony of moments lived with intention and perseverance. It is not the fireworks that illuminate the night sky briefly but the lighthouse that stands resilient, guiding ships home.

The spectrum of love's expressions may vary, from the most tender caresses to the fierce determination to surmount obstacles, but at the core, love is anchored by this twinship. If we aspire to glimpse love's eternal face—not solely carved by romance but by resilience—we must not relinquish the continuous dedication that commitment and Consistency necessitate.

As we conclude this meditation, let us affirm that love is not an accidental encounter nor a convenient emotion. It is a chosen path, a deliberate journey marked by the footprints of Commitment and Consistency. It leads not to a fleeting locale of satisfaction but to the enduring kingdom of shared service and sacrifice—the true essence of love's enduring power.

Tools for Nurturing a Sustained Love Within our grasp lies the ability to cultivate an enduring love that outlasts the initial flames of passion and settles into a warm, steady glow. The tools to forge such love are not preassembled; they must be fashioned with intention and care, beginning with a solid communication foundation.

Think of love as a garden - it requires consistent tending. To keep it flourishing, you must feed it with understanding, water it with patience, and prune it with wisdom. Active listening is the first tool you'll need in this garden of love. This is more than hearing words; it's about perceiving feelings and reading between the lines of a partner's speech. It calls for a heart tuned into empathy, respecting what is said and how it is expressed.

Another vital implement at your disposal is affectionate language. Words have the power to heal or harm. Kind utterances, gentle encouragement, and speaking in a love language that resonates with your partner can fortify your bonds. Words of affirmation act as sustenance, feeding the roots of your relationship and encouraging it to grow deeper and more robust.

Forgiveness is yet another essential tool, often overlooked, yet it's the very agent that can mend fences and clear thorny patches. Forgiveness shouldn't be seen as a weakness but as a courageous act of choosing love over the weight of grudges. Bearing forgiveness in your toolshed allows both of you to make mistakes, learn, and continue to thrive.

Patience is the soil in which love roots. Rushing the growth of love is akin to forcing a plant to bloom before its time; it can only lead to wilt. Exercise patience with your partner's imperfections and the natural progression of your relationship. Through patience, we understand that love's fruits mature sweetest when time is allowed to ripen.

Quality time, spent intentionally, acts as sunlight, illuminating the best aspects of each other and sparking joy in shared experiences. Whether it's a quiet evening walk, cooking a meal together, or engaging in a hobby, this shared time stands against the forces that would drive you apart.

Joining quality time is the instrument of shared goals and dreams. Planning a future together—with room for individual growth—gives love a direction to advance. It's like setting coordinates for a voyage; whether you navigate smooth or choppy waters, you're in it together, striving for common horizons.

Humor and laughter could be likened to rain that washes away sorrow and distress. It breaks the monotony, lightens the burden, and has a miraculous way of bringing hearts closer. Infusing your relationship with laughter is like adding a spontaneous melody that makes every shared moment more memorable.

Physical touch should not be undervalued; a tender touch, a heartfelt hug, or a reassuring hand squeeze can speak volumes. Our skin is a canvas; through touch, we can paint comfort, security, and passion, drawing a masterpiece that resonates with the soul's yearning for connection.

Gratitude is the mulch that protects the roots of love from the freezing chill of entitlement. Expressing sincere thanks for your partner's actions and their presence in your life reinforces the value you both bring to the table. It prevents the growth of bitterness and nurtures the blooms of appreciation.

A tool like conflict resolution skills can be life-saving in times of conflict. Addressing issues with a solution-oriented mindset rather than a fault-finding one ensures that your love remains healthy and that disagreements become opportunities for growth rather than roadblocks.

Then, there's the scaffold of support, standing firm when winds of hardship swirl. Knowing you can lean on each other, that your partner will be there to support your ambitions and comfort you through grief, creates a sanctuary from life's relentless pace. It builds resilience in the face of adversity.

Emotional and physical intimacy is the treasure at the end of the garden. It's where honesty, vulnerability, and passion intertwine, creating a sacred space where love's mysteries are unveiled. Cultivating intimacy requires a delicate balance, a give and take that honors both your needs and your partner's.

Also, the continuous pursuit of personal growth enriches any relationship. Expanding your boundaries brings new energy and perspectives back to the relationship, keeping the dynamic evolving and exciting. Love does not thrive on stagnation but flourishes with fresh flows of insight and self-improvement.

Anchoring all these tools is commitment, the unspoken promise that you choose to stay and work towards a shared future in the face of fleeting emotions and life's uncertainties. It signifies that love is beyond serving one's own needs; it's a joint expedition, bound by the decision to put 'us' before 'I.'

When wielded with love and awareness, all these tools create an environment where love can survive and thrive. Sustained love is not a mythical narrative; it's a transformative journey that refines us, making us wiser, kinder, and more connected to the essence of our humanity. Embrace these tools, and you shape not just a relationship but a legacy of love.

Chapter 15:
Synthesizing the Metamorphosis of Love

As our journey approaches its twilight, let us hold the essence of love like a luminous ember in our hands, feeling its warmth and contemplating its constant transformation. Love, as explored, is not merely a fleeting set of emotions, nor is it defined by the glorious acts that literature and media often glorify. It's a rich tapestry woven with the threads of understanding, empathy, sacrifice, and, above all, an enduring commitment to serve one another genuinely.

Throughout the chapters of this exploration, we've come to recognize that societal expectations often shroud the true face of love in a veil of idealization. To truly grasp the scope of love, we've looked beyond the whims of culture and time, drawing upon the wisdom latent within the sonnets and scriptures that have transcended generations.

The philosophy and literature surrounding love have illustrated its permanence and evolution across human history. As we've seen, love is not an artifact to be observed from afar but rather an ever-shifting spectrum of connection and growth, adaptable to the ages yet unwavering in its fundamental nature.

In the critical assessment of self-love and narcissism, we've explored the tender balance between caring for oneself and the trap of self-absorption. Through this lens, we've seen how the beam of self-regard can guide us toward nourishing our capacity for love without pouring into the chasm of ego.

Furthermore, we've delved into the heart of compassionate love and its expressions of altruism and empathy. Scientific inquiry has only reinforced what some of the greatest thinkers and poets have mused upon—the transformative power of putting compassion into practice.

Our inquiry into whether love is a feeling or an act of serving has led us to an inevitable conclusion. Love, in its most profound manifestation, is both. It's the emotion that propels us forward and the conscious choice to serve that sustains our journey through the peaks and valleys of life.

Indeed, love's lifecycle is not linear but cyclical—a testament to the persevering quality of love through stages of infatuation, challenges, and the rewarding terrain of mature, deep connection.

The foundational role of communication cannot be understated in our synthesis. Words, coupled with the intention to listen authentically, forge the backbone of love—a love that can withstand the tremors of misunderstandings and conflict.

It's within the realm of challenges where love is tested and, more importantly, where it grows. Overcoming obstacles strengthens our bonds, enriching our understanding of love's resilience and our capacity for forgiveness and growth.

As we consider the creation of a lasting bond, we turn our thoughts towards commitment and consistency. It's not the grand declarations of love that build an enduring connection, but rather the daily acts of love, respect, and dedication that cement this bond.

The metamorphosis of love is perhaps most evident in the realization that it is a decision, a vow renewed with each dawn. Love's myriad expressions, from the silent comfort of presence to the clamorous sacrifice of one's desires for another's welfare, illustrate its transformative power in our lives.

We arrive now at the heart of our synthesis, understanding that love is multi-faceted and singular, encompassing a myriad of expressions yet converging on one truth: love is transformative. It's an alchemy that turns ordinary into extraordinary, melding two souls in the crucible of shared existence.

And so, we must recognize that love, in its true form, is not a mere emotion to be sought and captured. It is a dynamic force that demands our active participation, a choice to serve, and to be served in the cyclical dance of giving and receiving.

In concluding this exploration of love's metamorphosis, may we carry forward the understanding that love is as much about the brilliance of shared joy as it is about the silent fortitude in times of grief. Love is the courage to remain vulnerable and the strength to grow impenetrable together. It is the gentle whisper of support and the roaring cry of shared victories. It is voluntary service characterized by a consistent, persistent, prolonged, and sustained commitment, investing in others and ensuring their well-being is achieved and maintained.

Ultimately, love is the essence of humanity's most incredible quest—the pursuit of a connection that transcends the self to find a sublime unity with another. It is the metamorphosis of two lives independently extraordinary, synthesizing into a harmony more significant than the sum of its parts. We now understand that love's accurate measure is not in the fleeting highs of passion but in the sustained symphony of serving one another through every note of life's complex composition.

Appendix A:
Research on Longevity in Relationships

As we have journeyed through understanding the nature of love and the forces that drive us toward deep, meaningful connections, it's vital that we also explore the science behind long-lasting relationships. What compels two individuals to weather the storms of life together, to intertwine their paths so intricately that the passage of time only cements their bond?

This appendix is a synthesis of research and findings related to the perseverance and resilience of love over time. A heartfelt bond can stand against the relentless tide of challenges and emerge stronger, driven by an undercurrent of mutual support, unwavering trust, and shared growth.

Fundamentals of Relationship Longevity

Effective Communication: The cornerstone of a durable relationship is the ability to share openly, listen actively, and resolve conflicts with compassion. A harmonious exchange of words is an art form that partners refine over time.

Respect and Appreciation: Mutual respect is a non-negotiable aspect of lasting love. Appreciation, conveyed through small gestures and understanding, can significantly enhance emotional bonds.

Shared Goals: Common objectives and dreams create a sense of unity, guiding a couple as they navigate life's labyrinth together.

Flexibility and Adaptability: Change is a given, but how partners adapt and support each other through transformation is crucial in sustaining a relationship.

These components don't merely exist; they are actively pursued and cherished. Through the conscious choice to serve the relationship, partners foster an enduring love—one that shifts, matures, and consistently renews itself.

Delving into Longevity

Long-term studies have revealed patterns that successful couples often exhibit, including a deep friendship at the base of their romantic connection.

Shared rituals and traditions can be anchors, providing a predictable and comforting pattern to a couple's life together.

Overcoming adversity offers opportunities for growth and strengthening. Resilient couples draw closer when faced with a crisis, using the hardship to reinforce their partnership.

At its core, the journey of a lasting partnership is marked by consistent nurturance. It's not merely luck that keeps the flame alive but a delicate dance of mutual efforts—small, everyday choices that, compounded over time, construct an unshakeable foundation.

Exploring the depth and breadth of this research, we recognize patterns and practices that transcend mere infatuation and touch upon the true essence of a durable bond. The secrets to relationship longevity lie in the subtle art of giving more than we take, serving without expecting, and honoring the sanctity of a shared life.

Conclusion

To love is to brave the journey of growth together, tenderly crafting a mutual narrative that survives the ebb and flow of life. This research bears the truth that relationship longevity is neither an accident nor a mystery. It is the fruit of labor, the consequence of choosing, day after day, to embed oneself in the spirit of service to the union. In serving, we discover the greatest depths of feeling, and the beautiful paradox of love manifests in this.

Appendix B:
Love in Action - Volunteering and Community Service

Going deeper into our understanding of love, we arrive at a powerful intersection of emotion and action. When love transforms from a mere sentiment into a demonstrable effort to improve the lives around us, volunteering and community service stand as its actual embodiments. In a society that often equates love with a whirlwind of emotions, the roots of more profound social love lie in the silent but persistent acts of serving others. This assertion compels us to reflect on how love manifests not only in the thrall of passion or the bonds of family and friendship but in the broader scope of human connection.

Venturing into the realm of community service, we uncover a terra firma where love is not proclaimed through grand gestures but through countless hours of selfless work. Regardless of the cause, whether feeding food-insecure individuals or tutoring children, these are the arenas where love is deeply felt and rarely spoken. Here, volunteers embody a commitment to a love that acts and heals, listening to the unvoiced needs of those they serve.

The Silent Ripples of Compassion

Within the heart of every community are individuals whose hands are full from digging into the real issues that afflict their neighbors. Their work is often unnoticed by the media and uncelebrated by the masses. Yet, precisely, this type of love in action molds the character of societies and cultures. It's a love that doesn't seek recognition but is content in the quiet acknowledgment of lives touched and improved. This is the love that builds playgrounds in desolate areas and revives community centers on the brink of closure. The love that knows no bounds nor discriminates—it reaches out to all in need.

A Call to Serve

In contemplating love as a service, one might be reminded that to love our neighbors is not just a sentimental wish but an active pursuit. Offering one's time and talents to the community is an open invitation to all, beckoning those willing to serve. These opportunities forge connections between people from disparate walks of life, breaking down barriers. Each act of service becomes a thread in the exquisite tapestry of communal love, teaching us that we belong to each other in more profound ways than we might have imagined.

The Reverberations of Altruistic Love

When we align our actions with our compassionate instincts, volunteering becomes a form of altruism that resonates far beyond the immediate act. It's a testament to the enduring impact of love in action. By caring for the well-being of another, we are offering a silent ode to the interconnectedness of human spirits. In doing so, we not only aid others but nurture the growth of our hearts, realizing that in giving ourselves, we receive immeasurable warmth and fulfillment.

The chapters before this one have dissected and parsed love's philosophical underpinnings, its societal interpretations, and the personal journey through emotional ebbs and flows. However, without the practical application demonstrated through volunteering and community service, the concept would float in theoretical space, untethered to the real-world embodiment of love's most authentic form. In these expressions, love is seen as serving and touching individuals and communities with its transformative power, urging us to look beyond our own narratives and write new ones of collective upliftment and support.

Thus, as we ponder the path of love and its multifaceted nature, let us remember love's profound capability for action. It reassures us that, in giving oneself and offering one's time, expertise, and care, we are participating in an eternal cycle of love that transcends immediate gratification and ushers in a sustained, lasting legacy of compassion and human connectivity. This is love in its most glorious form – love in action.